DECENTRALISATION IN DEVELOPING COUNTRIES

DECENTRALISATION IN DEVELOPING COUNTRIES

S.S. MEENAKSHISUNDARAM
Indian Administrative Service

CONCEPT PUBLISHING COMPANY, NEW DELHI 110059

ISBN 81-7022-521-3

First Published 1994

Published and Printed by
Ashok Kumar Mittal
Concept Publishing Company
A/15-16, Commercial Block, Mohan Garden
NEW DELHI-110059 (India)

Lasertypeset by
Printing Express
H-13, Bali Nagar
NEW DELHI-110015

PREFACE

This book is an analysis of an on-going process of people's participation in public governance. By a strange coincidence I handled the subject of decentralised governance first at the level of a State and then at the Centre, in the world's largest democracy – India. As the Secretary to Government of Karnataka in-charge of Rural Development and Panchayati Raj, I was lucky to be an integral part of the team that undertook an exercise to decentralise power from the State to the locally elected Panchayati Raj Institutions (PRIs) in Karnataka during 1986-1989. I then participated in the passing of the Constitution (73rd Amendment) Act, 1992 providing constitutional status to the Panchayats, when I came over to New Delhi to serve as Joint Secretary in the Government of India, in the Ministry of Rural Development. The experience gained in these two tenures by actually handling the ticklish issues relating to decentralisation and the exposure I had by studying the decentralised patterns in two other countries – Nigeria and the People's Republic of China (PRC) – which are quite comparable to India in many respects, have given me the courage to attempt this narration.

I am grateful to Prof. James Manor of the Institute of Development Studies (IDS), Sussex, United Kingdom, who has been largely responsible for inducing me to take up this study. Without his active cooperation, I would not have undertaken this study covering three different countries each of which have a large area and substantial population. The field visits and the research leading to the findings of this study were undertaken during my visiting fellowship at the IDS, Sussex, during 1990-91.

I am indebted to the Ford Foundation, New York, who, I understand, had generously funded the IDS, Sussex, for undertaking this study and more particularly to Shri R. Sudarshan of the Ford Foundation, New Delhi for the excellent support extended in organising my field visits. I am indeed grateful to Shri T.R. Satishchandran, the then Director of the Institute of Social and Economic Change, Bangalore, who had taken the trouble of going through the manuscripts of this book very thoroughly and suggested improvements wherever required.

The study would not have been possible without the active support and cooperation of many individuals, groups and institutions. Though each of them deserve a separate mention, the sheer length of the list that would have to be drawn up deters me from doing so. I must however make a specific mention of Mr. Halidu Abubaker, Head of the Department of Local Government Studies, Institute of Administration, Ahmadu Bello University, Zaira and Mr. Wang zhen Yao, Chief of the Countryside Division in the Department of Grassroots organs of State Power, Ministry of Civil Affairs, PRC, for having made the task of my study smooth and purposeful in Nigeria and PRC respectively. I am deeply indebted to the villagers in different parts of Nigeria, PRC and India who participated with great zeal and enthusiasm in the discussions I had with them and to the officials and Non-Government Agencies who arranged for these meethings at short notice.

The main purpose of my writing this book is to initiate a meaningful discussion on the powers, responsibilities and the functions that can be entrusted to the PRIs. Following the failure of national planning and rule through centralised institutions in different countries, there is a favourable climate now for decentralisation throughout the developing world. India, as a torch-bearer of this new development has recently passed a bold legislation conferring constitutional status to the elected local bodies. This experiment can succeed only if adequate powers and responsibilities are given both in letter and spirit, to the local institutions. If this book can generate ideas which can result in the emergence of a healthy system of local governance throughout the developing world, I would be more than satisfied.

S.S. MEENAKSHISUNDARAM

CONTENTS

1

INTRODUCTION

When I joined the Government of Karnataka, a peace-loving State in southern India, as their secretary incharge of the Rural Development and Panchayati Raj Department during the summer of 1986, I never imagined that I was going to be an integral part of an interesting exercise through which the State power was decentralised in favour of the locally elected district rural governments. Though the implementation of the decentralisation plan, that was politically conceived, was the broad brief given to me when I took charge, I came to be intimately involved not only in creating suitable local institutions and assigning to them resources, functions and personnel, but also in dealing with the management problems in their early days of establishment, owing to an act of Providence.[1] Through the professional handling of an essentially democratic exercise, I got interested in its theory and started learning more about the different patterns of decentralisation that were already going on in several parts of India, their relative merits and performance. Gradually the horizon was extended to cover larger areas outside India as well.

It is again a matter of coincidence that on my deputation to serve the Central Government at New Delhi, which most civil servants do at least once in their career, I have the good fortune of being the Joint Secretary incharge of decentralised governance. In that capacity, I witnessed the passing of the Constitution (Seventy Second Amendment) Bill by both the Houses of the Indian Parliament, in December 1992, endowing the Panchayats throughout India with the powers and authority to function as institutions of local self-government. I now have the responsibility of ensuring that the intentions of the Parliament are translated into action, throughout the country, which promises to be another interesting experience.

The environment at present, for a comparative study of decentralisation, is extremely congenial. Admittedly the concepts of nationally planned development and rule by the people through centralised institutions were largely the contribution of the East European Bloc to the developing world. The current counter-revolutionary trends in Eastern Europe, which rest mainly upon their economic failure, evidenced by poverty and inequality, inefficiency, corruption and insensitivity of the centralised bureaucracy and resentment against the arrogance of party elites, and the consequent rejection of the authoritarian rule in those countries have generated a favourable climate for decentralisation in the developing world as well. During the latter half of the 1980s, there has been a noticeable tendency to decentralise in a number of developing countries, whose limited experiences need to be documented.

Are attempts to compare political systems and administrative structures of any real value, especially if we are studying areas that seem primarily of national concern, which too must be adjusted to a local environment? It is true that historical and cultural factors have an impact on the extent and pattern of decentralisation in any country, or for that matter, the political and administrative structures even at the national level. However, in my view, a comparative study becomes useful as interdependencies grow between States and as issues, once considered essentially national in character, take on international importance. My study leads me to believe that common strands and patterns join all local government systems, and that by identifying such features, national systems can be made more productive if one has the willingness to learn from others. The main objective of this work, to put it briefly, is to examine a few models of decentralisation, compare them on a set of common parameters such as the environment in which the local units operate, the role they are expected to play and the resources they have at their disposal, and draw conclusions which can generate further discussion and research, more detailed and penetrating. I must admit that to identify trends and problem areas in one State in a period of transition is difficult enough, but to provide a comparable survey over so wide a range of countries is certainly a Herculean task and I would, therefore, request the reader to bear this limitation in mind.

We shall first take a brief look at the concepts of "decentralisation", "democracy" and "local governments", which are essential to this study. As I am neither a student of political science nor a practising politician, the discussions may tend to be more practical than academic and if this is a limitation, it may have to be forgiven.

Decentralisation

It is impossible to standardise the usage of the word "decentralisation" by seeking to give it meanings that would be acceptable universally. The English language, I understand, took the word from Latin and it has innumerable applications. Through all of them, however, runs a common idea, which is inherent in the word's Latin roots, meaning "away from centre".[2] To some, decentralisation denotes "the transference of authority, legislative, judicial or administrative, from a higher level of government to a lower level".[3] The process of decentralisation basically seeks to create greater energy, a higher sense of responsibility and better morale among the field agents.[4] Although the basic idea of decentralisation is sharing the decision-making authority with lower levels in the organisation, power can be shared within the system, at a lower level, or by creating new mechanisms in the system. Power can also be shared with outside organisations or agencies.

Keeping these possibilities in view, some authors[5] indicate the following four types of decentralisation:

(a) *deconcentration*, i.e. handing over some amount of administrative authority or responsibility to lower levels within the government ministries or agencies;
(b) *delegation*, i.e. transferring responsibility for specifically defined functions to organisations that are outside the regular bureaucratic structure and are only indirectly controlled by the Central Government;
(c) *devolution*, i.e. creation and strengthening of sub-national units of the government, activities of which are substantially outside the direct control of the Central Government; and
(d) *privatisation*, i.e. passing all responsibility for functions to non-governmental organisations or private enterprises independent of the government.

I would agree with the view that deconcentration denotes "more delegation to a subordinate officer of capacity to act in the name of the superior without a real transfer of authority"[6] and delegation refers to "relations in which powers are formally conferred under law on an executive agency or by an administrative order to a subordinate or from one level of government to another",[7] where again there is no real transfer of authority. Through the process of "privatisation", some governments have no doubt divested themselves of responsibilities for functions and have either transferred them to voluntary organisations and cooperatives or allowed them to be performed by private enterprises. But in most of these instances, governments continue to exercise some amount of supervision and support. At the margin, the distinction between privatisation and delegation is blurred.

Devolution, on the other hand, refers to the process of "the legal conferring of powers to discharge specified or residual functions upon a formally constituted local authority".[8] "It is not infrequently", rightly comments the study team on Community Projects and National Extension Service (appointed by the Government of India in 1957), "that delegation of power is mistaken for decentralisation. The former does not divest the government of the ultimate responsibility for the actions of the authority to whom power is delegated; this authority is under the control of the government and is in every way subordinate to it. Decentralisation, on the other hand, is a process whereby the government divests itself completely of certain duties and responsibilities and devolves them on to some other authority".[9] Decentralisation thereby creates a corporate sense of responsibility in local decision-making agencies with more or less independent existence and powers. "It is a training in self-government. It confines the administration of powers to those who will feel most directly the consequences of those powers".[10]

The word "decentralisation", at least in this book, will, therefore, relate to the devolution of powers resulting from the creation of bodies separated by law from the national centre in which local representatives are given formal power to decide on a range of public matters. Their political base is the locality and not – as it is with the commissioners and civil servants – the nation. Their area of authority is limited, but within that area their right to make decisions is entrenched by the law and can be altered only by new legislation. They have resources which, subject to the stated limit, are spent and invested at their own discretion.[11] This is the meaning of "decentralisation" as used in this book. A decentralised local body, in this sense, would have a separate legal existence, its own budget and the authority to allocate substantial resources on a range of different functions, and decisions would be made by the representatives of the local people, who constitute the body.

Decentralisation, being the process of sharing power, especially the decision-making authority, has to be a continuum from centralisation to full autonomy. The continuum will constitute the phases of decentralisation in a given country. The main decisions are to be made in relation to the tasks of a system or in relation to the resources to accomplish the tasks. Hence one can think of decentralisation as a continuum of controls of three variables: organisational tasks, finance and human resources. Tasks of control or autonomy may relate to policy-making, strategy formulation, planning, priority setting and implementation of programme. In financial and human resources, the concern of autonomy can relate to generation and procurement of resources, controlling and owning them and their utilisation.[12]

Why is decentralisation so important? An administrator or political leader at the centre can always say that the scarce resources of a developing nation can be used most efficiently and economically only if they are concentrated under a central authority and utilised through a national development plan by a national administration (sometimes a single political party perhaps). He may also suggest that the regional or ethnic differences within a nation are so powerful that, if given autonomy, they may break up the nation. This is a commonly held view which must be respected because it contains much that is simple commonsense. But it also leaves a few critical questions unanswered and it ignores the actual experience of attempts at centralised planning and control in many countries which ended up with an uncontrolled urban growth, a stagnating countryside, a gross national product whose increase fell far short of expectations and the consequent abandonment of the development plans!

On the other hand, it is possible to argue that ethnic and other factors which result in a pluralistic society make decentralisation all the more necessary if the unity and integrity of the country is to be maintained. A share in decision-making strengthens the bond between the different ethnic communities living within a nation, instead of breaking it up. Secondly, even within the administration, any official can quote examples of centralised decision-making that was wasteful or ineffective: the funds and supplies that never arrived, the projects that remained paper proposals, the approvals that could not be obtained unless one had a friend or relative in the central ministry. The experience gained in working a centralised system makes one realise the importance of decentralisation.

It was indeed the concept of centralisation that led to an alternative approach to problems of development which laid stress not so much on planned allocation of resources, but on winning support from the populations who were supposed to be "developed". This approach believes in the dictum that "people cannot be developed, they can only develop themselves". This states that people will change only if they understand and consent to the changes that are proposed -- never just because they receive orders from above. Government officials may know far more than the local people about the technology available, but the people know more about the environmental constraints of their own situations.

The official is often seen as a stranger on the local scene; he may not speak the local language and he enjoys a totally different lifestyle. How can he then take decisions on behalf of peasant farmers, involving hardships and risks for them? This was the rationale for most of the attempts to use representative local bodies in the development process.

Local Government

The United Nations Division of Public Administration defines a local government as "a political subdivision of a nation (or, in a federal system, a State) which is constituted by law and has substantial control of local affairs, including the powers to impose taxes or to extract labour for prescribed purposes. The governing body of such an entity is elected or otherwise locally selected . . . ."[13] This definition makes it clear that a local government is a lower-level government, when compared to a National or State Government; it is set up by law and has certain responsibilities; it is normally elected. Hugh Whalen makes some additions such as territory, population and legal identity, when he said that "each unit of local government in any system is assumed to possess the following characteristics, a given territory and population, an institutional structure . . . a separate legal entity, a range of powers and functions authorised by delegation from the appropriate central or intermediate legislature and lastly within the ambit of such delegation, autonomy subject always . . . to the test of reasonableness".[14]

Some of my colleagues not only in the Indian Administrative Service but also from the technical services strongly believe that elected local governments are a dispensable part of the democratic process, that it belongs to a specifically English political culture and that it is unreasonable to transplant it to a developing country. In my view, certain basic political mechanisms dictate themselves by their own logic. They are not culture specific. An elected local government appears to be one such. We seek to achieve four things in a local government through the mechanism of local participation. First, the ordinary local citizen should feel that he is not just an inert subject of an arbitrary government far removed from him, but a person whose views must be considered since the local government belongs to him and the ruler exists for his benefit and not the other way round. Second, the choice as to who rules them should be made by the local people themselves, as they are likely to choose the one who cares for their interests. Third, the local ruler should bear in mind the need to be sensitive to the local needs and articulate their needs so that he may continue to enjoy their local support. Fourthly, the local participation should provide the momentum for faster development through the harnessing of local resources. None of these benefits can be attributed either to a nominated local government or to the bureaucracy representing a distant government.

Local governments, though popular, may not always produce the results that the national leaders were hoping for. Elected councillors could be ignorant and self-seeking, lacking a sense of responsibility to their electors. They may usually concentrate on expanding the social services to the neglect of investments in productivity. The local government bureaucracy may be of poor quality, frequently losing control over their own accounting system. Local autonomy may lead to multiple frictions between the centre and the local body. But, with these and other possible shortcomings, the mere existence of local democratic structures can be a contribution; people generally prefer them to direct administration, even where the elections only give power to existing local leaders. The central legislature in any country, however popularly constituted, can never replace the local genius of the people as an agency of devising local solutions to local problems. Locally elected councils can exercise greater surveillance over local officials than that exercised by the central legislature over the Central Government officials. A World Bank study,[15] therefore, concludes that "guarded optimism on the utility of decentralisation in developing countries is justified. This conclusion is warranted by the number of cases in which small but clear-cut improvements have occurred as the result of decentralisation programs."

Decentralisation has Two Virtues

So long as representative and democratic institutions capable of supplying the local interest, supervision and care cannot be created, it would not be possible to evoke local interest and excite local initiative in the field of development administration. Strictly speaking, the term "decentralisation" does not necessarily contain any democratic connotation, hence the adjective "democratic" is used to impart a special meaning to the term. Democratic decentralisation possesses two virtues: it is consistent with the democratic trend and it is also technically the most efficient method of formulation and execution of local projects. It is democratic in the sense that the source from which power is decentralised has its democratic base and the body to which power flows is also democratically organised.[16] Some, therefore, conclude that "democratic decentralisation is a political ideal and local self-government is its institutional form".[17] As Ensminger points out, "with democratic decentralisation the administrative orientation must shift quite completely from making decisions and issuing orders to helping the people make decisions through their Panchayats, cooperatives and Samithis".[18] Thus the scheme of decentralisation facilitates the combination of, and cooperation between, the official machinery of administration and the non-official leadership and control through the mechanism of local governments.

Role of Local Government

Other than being an instrument of democratic decentralisation, what else can a local government be? Firstly, a local government can be an effective weapon for channelling local pressures, articulating and aggregating local interests, which may not necessarily coincide with the ideas of Central Governments. It can thus provide a forum for political education not only for the party leadership but also for the general population, who would be able to appreciate the utility of this basic level of government. Secondly, a local government, because of its closeness to a location, can provide certain services far more efficiently than the Central Government. This, of course, presupposes the superior capacity of local people to understand and conduct their local affairs. Thirdly, a local government, with its superior local knowledge, can plan for its social, economic and manpower betterment far more efficiently than a national government. Fourthly, local government can ensure better accountability of public officials to the citizens, because of its nearness to the people. Finally, local government, by virtue of its position, can be an effective communication channel between the centre and the people, which can, in a way, ensure the effectiveness of the Central Government's actions as well.

In addition, a local government can also perform two indirect functions: firstly, it can prevent the emergence of alternative power centres, at the local level, that are usually not subjected to the influence and authority of the State; secondly, it can be used to decongest the government at higher level(s), thereby freeing national or provincial leaders from unnecessary involvement in local issues.

At this stage it must be re-emphasised that a decentralised government is, however, a semi-dependent organisation. It has some freedom to act without referring to the centre for approval, but its status is not comparable with that of a sovereign State. The powers of local government, and even its existence, flow from a decision of the National Parliament or a State Legislature and can be curtailed or cancelled when the former or the latter so decides. Authority is too small to pose any threat to the National or State Government, though a council dominated by the political opposition can at best serve as an irritant – which has sometimes been the reason for the government in power to step in and dissolve the council. But the value of this semi-dependent political body is that it provides an opportunity and a channel for a government to hold the dialogue with the masses – to influence them and to get the feedback from them. A healthy local government is perhaps one in which central and popular influence over decision-making are properly balanced.

Basic Questions

Is there any conflict between "democracy", "decentralisation" and "development" as the three basic goals of "democratic decentralisation"? Should local government institutions be treated purely as development and/or service agencies or a power structure, providing a hierarchical chain of political offices through which the actual political power can be exercised? Without the party lines, can these institutions serve the functions of democracy and development? What should be the functions of these bodies, the financial and human resources they need to fulfil these functions and their relationship with other levels of government?

Need for Comparative Study

Arising out of these questions is the need for this comparative study covering selected States in India, Nigeria and the People's Republic of China. The choice of India is obvious, not only because of my personal knowledge but also from a historical point of view. British India was ruled by a governor-general, under whom governors (or lieutenant-governors) ruled the provinces, and district officers, variously called collectors, district magistrates or deputy commissioners, the districts. Though a unitary system should have been accompanied by a high degree of centralisation, these rulers were given a great deal of latitude to do what they wanted, in many local matters. With the dawn of independence in 1947 the governor-general and governors were gradually replaced by democratically elected governments at the Centre and in the States. But the districts continued to be administered as before. A bureaucratically decentralised system thus gave way to a politically centralised one.[19]

The history of local governments (usually called Panchayati Raj institutions) in India goes back to over a century. It had its formal birth during the viceroyalty of Lord Rippon who established local self-government institutions such as municipal and district boards. Ironically it was after the advent of freedom that these institutions lost whatever powers they had. The first Prime Minister of India, Pandit Jawaharlal Nehru, gave a new thrust to the concept of local governments in the mid-1950s and ushered in a programme of democratic decentralisation through the Panchayati Raj institutions. (The expression Panchayati Raj was coined by Nehru himself, to give an Indian name to the English words "democratic decentralisation", according to Mr. S.K. Dey who, as the Union Minister for Community Development, was one of the key architects of the "Panchayati Raj" in India, after independence.)

Since then different State Governments in India have taken up different experiments in local government systems at different points of time, as local government is a subject allocated to State Governments under the Indian Constitution.[20] Five of them stand out prominently – the Western States of Maharashtra and Gujarat which had adopted almost similar models of decentralisation during the early 1960s, the eastern State of West Bengal which has been governed by the Marxist-led coalition for almost two decades now, and the southern States of Andhra Pradesh and Karnataka whose decentralisation models are distinctly different from the earlier ones. Karnataka, being the last in the series, had the advantage of looking at the experiences of the other States and frankly, while framing the Karnataka legislation on local governments during the early eighties, we helped ourselves with many ideas from the other models, most notably the West Bengal one. Most other States are now in the process of establishing their own local government structures, following the amendment to the Constitution of India, providing for the mandatory establishment of local governments throughout the country. Thus a comparative study of these models, by itself, can throw adequate light on the basic questions we raised about democratic decentralisation earlier.

Interestingly Africa too, over the past century, has set up a laboratory of experiments with various systems of local administration, in both colonial and post-colonial periods. Every form, from direct central administration to strongly autonomous local governments, has been tried in a mixture of different societies. The failure of one has been rapidly followed by trials of another. For some analysts of the subject, the African experience appears far richer than that provided by Asian countries, where the main hierarchy of administration is often more rigid and slower to change.[21] By far the most impressive implementation of decentralised local governments was the Nigerian experience begun by the military regime in 1975 and continued through the successive civil and military regimes. In his guidelines for the new construction, the then Head of State, Murtala Mohammed, urged the elimination of over-centralisation of power in a few hands and, as a matter of principle, "to decentralise power whenever possible, as a means of diffusing tension".[22] A set of national guidelines was issued, in 1976, for the reform of local governments and to strengthen the independence of these local governments, the office of the divisional officer, the kingpin of colonial administration at the local level, was abolished. Despite the change of governments, both civil and military, the concept of decentralisation was kept alive.

The new Nigerian Constitution (1989) once again guarantees the system of local governments by democratically elected local government councils. It establishes autonomous governments at two levels below the Centre – States and the local governments within them. Each tier has specifically protected powers and revenues that are allocated in advance by a formula to fund legislative policies. Establishment of democratically elected local government councils has been an integral part of the programme for a return to democracy in Nigeria, announced by its military rulers.

It is often said of Nigeria and, by extension, other countries in Africa, that it is really a collection of local communities and not a

State. That would suggest that decentralisation, on grounds of both effectiveness and democracy, should provide the most pragmatic form of government. Yet it was only centralised regimes – first the colonial administration, then the military – that instituted authentic local governments in Nigeria![23] This makes the study of local governments in Nigeria even more interesting.

Around the same period, to be precise in December 1978, there was a significant break in China's development policies, inasmuch as the "people's communes" which had played a key role in the economic, social and political life of rural China for over two decades abruptly lost their stronghold on the production activities and a key organisational change, called the "Production Responsibility System" was introduced. The new system aimed at stimulating peasant productivity by increasing the proportion of privately farmed land, diversifying agricultural production, allowing freer reign for household sideline production and expanding the role of rural markets. Because the essence of these innovations is to expand the role of markets and promote production by reducing the scope and intensity of direct government control at the level of the production unit, some classify these efforts as decentralisation.[24] At any rate, increasing lower-level autonomy, while decreasing the involvement of higher-level bureaucrats, can certainly be termed as deconcentration at least.

The effect of the "open policy" announced in December 1978, was the gradual disappearance of the "communes" and the establishment of township/town people's governments in their place. China now has recognised governments at three distinct levels below the Centre – province, county and township – even though the nomenclature may vary depending upon the urban or rural characteristics of the locality. The latest grassroot level organ is the village committee, which is a self-managed mass organisation, created by the village committee law which is under trial implementation in the People's Republic of China since June 1, 1988. The village committee is, however, not an organ of State power. The developments in China on the local government front during the past few years, culminating in the creation of village committees, especially in the spheres of economic development and financial resources, deserve a closer look.

Certain striking similarities between the three countries need to be mentioned at this stage, which make their systems comparable. They all have a very large area with a substantial population, around 80 per cent of whom live in villages. All three have vast and diverse natural resources which need to be tapped. They have a federal system of government with each region or province having its own individual identity, in the form of ethnicity, language and even culture. Interestingly the experiments that are to be discussed in this book were conceived during the latter half of the seventies – the local government reforms in Nigeria (1976), the open policy proclamation in China (1978) and the Ashok Mehta Committee report which revived the Panchayati Raj movement in India (1978) – and their implementation commenced in the latter half of the eighties – through the 1989 Constitution in Nigeria, the Village Committee Law (1988) in China and the Karnataka system of Panchayati Raj (1987). All these experiments are thus new and are yet to take root.

Though the elections have taken place once during December 1990, for all the 449 local governments in Nigeria, all of them have now been dissolved by the new Military regime, which however, promises to hold elections to these local governments once again. Whether the village committee will also become a regular constituent of the local government structure at the lowest level in China is still not clear. The Karnataka legislation, which was widely held as a far-reaching model on decentralised governance, has already been replaced by a less radical system by the successor government. It is thus obvious that these experiments have generated a lot of public and political interest in the respective countries. Democracy in India, the military regime in Nigeria and one-party rule in China provide differing environments to this interesting comparison of their local government systems.

This study involved my travelling to the countries concerned, in order to understand the historical background, the existing pattern and the resources that were being put into local governments in each one of them. As such, the study is based on the institutions operating at the local level and their relationship with the Central and State Governments. While there is a general dearth of literature on local government systems in Nigeria, the available material on China is almost entirely in Chinese, making it extremely difficult for a foreigner to make full use of. However, I was lucky to establish useful contacts with academicians and public servants in both these countries who helped me in getting a number of reports, reviews and also government statistics. This information was then supplemented by interviews and discussions with politicians, public servants and academicians who were quite willing to accommodate my requests even at short notice.

Since the terminology used varies from country to country and even within a country, there is a need to explain the terms used in this book to cover the systems of government under comparison. While the term Central or Federal Government will always represent the national government at the capital of the country, the term State or Provincial Government will mean the governments at the next lower level administering different States or Provinces within the country. The local government council in Nigeria, the county government in China or the Zilla Parishad or District Panchayat in India are the local governments at the next lower level of comparison. (Though Prefectures in China and Divisions in India represent an intermediate level between Province or State and county or district, there are no local governments at either of these levels.)

Usually a zilla or district in India is much bigger than an average local government area in Nigeria, or a county in China. While the local government area is the lowest tier in the Nigerian set-up, China has one more tier below the county called the township or town, with a local government attached to it. In India while some States have only one tier below the district called "mandal", many others have two tiers below the district called "taluk" or "block" and the village or group of villages. The words Panchayat and Panchayat Samiti in the Indian context always refer to a council elected or nominated to run the affairs of the local body at that level. Similarly the term "panchayati raj" is used to mean the entire local government structure below the State level in India. The words "scheduled caste" and "scheduled tribe" (SC and ST) in the Indian context always refer to the weakest sections of the caste-ridden Indian society. (There are around 160 million SC/ST people in India, accounting for about 20 per cent of her population.)

Finally, the arrangement of chapters in this work – the next two chapters deal with the local government systems in Nigeria and China, which are followed by a general description of the Indian scene first and then a detailed account of the Karnataka model in the next two chapters. I have attempted an analysis of the three systems under the common parameters of structure, functions and resources in the following three chapters. My impressions and conclusions form the last chapter of this work.

NOTES AND REFERENCES

1. Sri Abdul Nazir Sab, who was the Minister for Rural Development and Panchayati Raj in the Government of Karnataka during 1983-88 and who was the

chief architect of their decentralisation programme fell ill within one year of the introduction of the new system in April 1987, and ultimately passed away of lung cancer in October 1988. During his illness the task of sorting out the management problems of the new structure fell on this author who was the secretary in charge of the department at that time.

2. A.W. Macmakon, *Delegation and Autonomy*, Asia Publishing House, Bombay, 1961, p. 15.
3. Leonard D. White, "Decentralisation', *Encyclopaedia of Social Sciences*, Vol. 5, New York, Macmillan, 1959.
4. Ashok Kumar Mukhopadhyay, *The Panchayat Administration in West Bengal*. The World Press Private Limited, 1980, p. 5.
5. Rondenelli, D.A., J.R. Nellis and G.S. Cheema (1984). *Decentralisation in developing countries*, Washington, World Bank.
6. Leonard D. White, *op. cit.*
7. A.W. Macmakon, *op. cit.*, p. 16.
8. Henry Maddick, *Democracy, Decentralisation and Development*, Asia Publishing House, Bombay, 1966, p. 23.
9. *Report of the Team for the Study of Community Projects and National Extension Service, Committee on Plan Projects*, New Delhi, Vol. I, 1957, Sec. 2, p. 7.
10. Harold J. Laski, *A Grammar of Politics*, George Allen & Unwin London, 1960, p. 61.
11. Philip Mawhood, *Local Government in the Third World*, New York and Chichester, Willey, 1983.
12. Udai Pareek, *Decentralisation for Effective Governance*, Centre for Administrative Change, Jaipur, India. 1989, p. 2.
13. United Nations, *Summer Conference in Local Government in Africa*, Cambridge, 1961, p. 11.
14. Hugh Whalen, *Ideology, democracy and the foundation of local self-government*, Toronto Methuen, 1970, p. 312.
15. Rondenelli, D.A., J.R. Nellis and G.S. Cheema, *op. cit.*
16. A.K. Mukhopadhyay, *op. cit.*
17. Iqbal Narain, "The idea of democratic decentralisation", *Indian Journal of Political Science*, Vol. XXI, No. 2, (p 191.)
18. D. Ensminger, "Democratic Decentralisation — A new administrative challenge", *Indian Journal of Public Administration*, July-September 1961.
19. Nirmal Mukarji, "Decentralisation below the State level", *Economic and Political Weekly*, Vol. XXIV, No. 9, 1989.
20. The Constitution of India, 1950, Item 5. List 2.
21. Philip Mawhood, *The Politics of Decentralisation: Eastern Europe and Africa*, 1990.
22. Address by the Head of the Federal Military Government at the opening session of the Constitution Drafting Committee on Saturday, 18 October, 1975, Government Printer, Lagos, 1976
23. Philip Mawhood, "Local Government in the Third World", Chapter II, *op. cit.*
24. Rondenelli, D.A., J.R. Nellis and G.S. Cheema, *op. cit.*

2

NIGERIAN LOCAL GOVERNMENTS

The Federal Republic of Nigeria lies within the tropics, between latitudes 4 and 14 of the Equator and longitudes 3 and 14 east of the Greenwich Meridian. The country is bounded in the east by the Republic of Cameroun and in the west by the Republic of Benin. Nigeria's northern neighbour is Niger Republic and on the north eastern portion, it is bounded by Lake Chad. The Atlantic ocean forms the southern boundary of Nigeria. The country has an area of 923,768 square kilometres. The 1963 census put Nigeria's population officially at 55.6 million. However the estimated population in 1990 is around 90 million. The population is multi-ethnic with over 350 linguistic groups and over 2,000 ethnic groups.The dominant groups are Hausa/Fulani (north), Yoruba (west) and Igbo (east).

Nigeria is a creation of British colonialism. Before 1914, when the northern and southern Protectorates and the colony of Lagos were amalgamated into the Colony and Protectorate of Nigeria, the geographical area now called Nigeria was composed of numerous kingdoms, emirates and city States, each of which was completely independent of the other. The colonial State of Nigeria was imposed by the British rulers mostly to protect their own interests against rivalry from other European national capitalists.

History

The history of the Nigerian local government can be divided into six major periods, each one coinciding with a significant event in Nigeria's political history.[1] These are:

(a) the early colonial period from 1900 – 1952;
(b) the late colonial period/early Independence period from 1952-65;
(c) the first military regime from 1966-75;
(d) the second military regime from 1975-79;

(e) the Presidential civilian era from 1979-83; and
(f) the third military regime from 1984 onwards.

During the early colonial period, local government in Nigeria largely meant the local manifestation of the Central Government. Though the political institutions in different regions were structurally diverse, the central figure was a prefect, assisted and advised by qualified ex-patriate officers. Associated with them in a degree of relationship and responsibility so varied as to defy any generalisation were "native authorities". They varied from those commanding relatively substantial revenues and employing qualified staff to those whose resources were so minimal that their authority had little to do with development and was largely confined to traditional matters. It was in essence a French system of local government though the British colonial theory held it otherwise.[2] The system succeeded in the northern parts of the country where an elaborate and authoritarian form of emirates (areas governed by one traditional chief) already existed, but it was only partially successful in the west where the traditional institutions were more democratic and was a complete failure in the east where no such strong central institutions existed.[3]

As the demand for self-government reached its peak in the late 1940s, a period which coincided with the term of the Labour Government in Britain, each of the regions substituted British type three-tiered democratically elected local government system for the indirect rule system, the eastern region was the first (in 1950) and was followed by the western and northern regions in 1952 and 1954 respectively.

Though these experiments in local democracy could not succeed, the principles they represented, namely, integration of traditional chiefs into local administration and the integration of local government administration into Central and State administration, continued to engage the attention of the policy makers in Nigeria. When the military came to power in 1966, therefore, one of the first things they did was to dissolve all the local government councils and replace them with management committees comprising officials and a few hand-picked members. Several reforms were proposed and most significantly in the mid-west and the eastern States, local governments were absorbed into the State bureaucracy in what was then known as development administration. The local councils became mere advisory committees to the field units of the central departments with a drastic reduction in their powers and finances and thus in their effectiveness. This in part formed the background to the nation-wide reform of local governments in 1976 by the new military administration that came to power in July, 1975, with a pledge to return the country to civilian administration within four years. The reorganisation of local administration was on the top of their agenda as they genuinely felt that a strong representative local government system was a pre-condition for the return to democracy at the national level.

An important aspect of the 1976 reforms was the termination of the development administration system and the creation of single-tiered local authorities all over the country. "The guidelines for local government reform in Nigeria" which forms the basic document for the reform does reveal the intention of the Central Government to constitute a distinct level of local government with definite boundaries and reasonably well-stated functions. These reforms revived the interest in local governments throughout the country and the increasing demand that followed for more councils all over the country is itself a testimony to their achievement.

The major developments since the return to civilian rule in 1979 have been the steep increase in the number of local governments from 301 at the end of the military administration in 1979 to over 700 by March, 1982, and the enactment of a Revenue Allocation Law in 1982 which set aside 10 per cent of the federation account and 10 per cent of State revenues as statutory transfer to local governments. With the large number of councils, there was an inevitable reduction in the finances and technical personnel available to local governments. There were also instances of State Governments diverting federal grants to other areas of priority overlooking the needs of the local governments. Many local governments did not have duly elected members since 1979 in view of the delays in the compilation of new electoral list by the Federal Electoral Commission. Hence, when the military struck again on December 31, 1983, they had to set things right and as a first step, they reverted the local governments to their 1979 position and the number of local governments was reduced to the original 301.

On the whole, the developments since 1984 indicate more continuity than change. A committee was established in 1984 to review local government administration in the country against the background of the major reform initiative embarked upon in 1976.[4] Pending the completion of the committee's work and the adoption of a new policy guideline, the management of the country's 301 local governments was entrusted to State Government officials called "sole administrators".

Although the sole administrator system proved efficient and effective in respect of revenue collection and maintenance of law and order,[5] it was in a sense the very antithesis of local democracy and whatever development activities were embarked upon, they were "top down" rather than "bottom up". Hence the sole administrator system was given up after about 30 months by the new Babangidda administration which came to power in 1985 and replaced by a local government council made up of an administrator who served as a full-time chairman, and four other members who were appointed from among the citizens of each local government area to serve on a part-time basis as an interim measure.

Though elections to local governments were held in December 1987/March 1988, the need to clearly spell out the role of the local government *vis-a-vis* the Central and State Governments under the administration's plan of return to civilian rule by 1992 remained. In addition, there were mounting demands for the creation of more local governments in several parts of the country. With the ostensible motive of preventing the present incumbents from getting any undue advantage of office in an electoral battle to be held on party basis, the elected local governments were once again dissolved, a local government (basic constitutional and transitional provisions) decree, establishing *inter alia* 449 local government areas in Nigeria, was promulgated in May 1989, and elections were held on that basis to the local governments during December 1990. To a large extent, the present system of local government in Nigeria is thus based on the 1976 local government reforms as modified by the Constitution of the Federal Republic of Nigeria 1989 (hereafter, the 1989 Constitution) whose provisions came into force on October 1, 1992.

Structure

The national guidelines for the 1976 local government reforms define a local government in Nigeria as "government at local level exercised through representative councils established by law to exercise specific powers within defined areas. These powers should give the council substantial control over local affairs as well as the staff and institutional and financial powers to initiate and direct the provision of services and to determine and implement projects so as to complement the activities of the State and Federal Governments in their areas, and to ensure, through devolution of functions to these councils and through the active participation of the people and the traditional institutions, that local initiative and response to local needs and conditions are maximised".[6] The essence of this long-winded definition is that the local governments will complement the activities of the higher level governments in so far as they relate to the local area, by providing services and implementing the projects. They will have the necessary control over local resources, for this purpose. The representative character of the local government council is expected to maximise local initiative and public participation in the development activities of the governments.

This definition is amplified, while indicating the principal aims of the local government, namely, "(a) to make appropriate services and development activities responsive to local wishes and initiatives by devolving or delegating them to local representative bodies; (b) to facilitate the exercise of democratic self-government close to the local levels of our society and to encourage initiative and leadership potential; (c) to mobilise human and material resources through the involvement of members of the public in their local development; (d) to provide a two-way channel of communication between local communities and government (both State and Federal)".[7]

Under the 1989 Constitution the system of local governments by democratically elected local government councils has been guaranteed.[8] The inclusion of a whole chapter (Chapter 8) in the new Constitution clearly signifies the creation of local government as the acknowledged third tier of the government in Nigeria. The local governments are designed to be multi-purpose, single-tier institutions with definite boundaries, powers and resources established under State legislation and with functions for which they are responsible to the State.

Though the government of a State can, by law, create, for any local government area, up to a maximum of seven development areas having regard to such factors as common, historical and traditional ties, geographical contiguity and administrative expedience[9], these areas do not constitute a separate tier as they entirely derive their funds by allocations from the parent local governments and discharge such functions as may be delegated to them by the parent bodies. The local governments, though designed to correspond to the Federal constituencies in such a way that no State would have more local governments than the number of Federal constituencies in that State, also satisfy by and large the conditions indicated in the 1976 reforms, namely, that each local government should serve a population between

150,000 and 800,000 with no upper limit for a major town which need not be split because of its large population.[10] Only the National Assembly has the power to create new local governments and a stringent procedure has in fact been spelt out in the 1989 Constitution for creating such new councils.[11]

Each local government area has been divided into such number of wards, not more than 20, as may be necessary and each local government council will have a directly elected chairman and a vice-chairman in addition to the councillors elected one each.[12] From among these councillors the chairman will have to appoint not less than three and not more than five supervisory councillors who may be allocated with the portfolios of finance and economic planning, works, education, health and other social services [13] The local government councils have a term of three years in office within which any councillor or the chairman or the vice-chairman can be recalled by the electorate – though the procedure prescribed for such a recall is quite cumbersome.[14] Though no provision exists in the Constitution enabling the State to dissolve an elected council in the event of any mismanagement, it is more than possible that the States may include such a provision in their own enactments (providing for the structure, composition and other matters relevant to the local governments in their State).

A unique feature of the Nigerian system, which does not obtain in India nor in China, is the role of traditional rulers or native authorities. Unlike in India where the erstwhile rulers were done away with at the time of the merger of their States with the independent Indian Union, Nigeria had not opted for the total annihilation of the traditional rulership. There are generally two ways of approaching the problem of the traditional rulers. One is the anthropological approach of treating these people as museum specimens to be observed and written about and not as living human beings with whom one could work. The other is of rather ignoring that they are something special and different and trying to absorb them into the normal pattern of society. Apparently the Nigerian rulers did not agree with either of these approaches and wanted to retain the traditional rulers as a useful link with the local people not only in religious matters but also in other fields of government activity. With the result, the Emir or the Paramount Chief, as he is called in Nigeria, is still a public man, with an Emirate or traditional council attached to him. Part II of the Fourth Schedule of the 1989 Constitution envisages an advisory role to the traditional council and makes it clear that "nothing in this schedule shall be construed as conferring any executive, legislative or judicial powers on a traditional council". The Emirs receive automatically copies of all agenda, supporting documents, notes and minutes of all local government councils within their area and can give general advice to the local government councils concerned, though such an advice need not always be binding.

Between the two possible approaches, namely, the traditionalisation of modern local governments by giving a pre-eminent position to the traditional ruler within the local government, and the modernisation of traditional rulership in line with the spirit of local governments, the 1989 Constitution has thus chosen the latter course.[15] Traditional rulers now exist only as extensions of local governments which can, however, delegate a number of functions revolving around support for art and culture, chieftaincy matters, determination of customary law and determination of religious matters to them for execution. The financial contributions from local governments to the traditional councils will be decided by the State Governments and will be mandatory on the local governmnets,[16] indicating the special role assigned to the traditional council *vis-a-vis* the local government.

Functions

The functions which the local governments are expected to perform can be broadly classified as those, "(a) which require detailed local knowledge for efficient performance; (b) in which success depends on community responsiveness and participation; and (c) which are of a personal nature requiring provision close to where the individuals affected live and in which significant use of discretion or understanding of individuals is needed, provided the services can be effectively rendered on the scale of a local government area".[17] Part One, under the Fourth Schedule of the 1989 Constitution, details the following as the main functions of a local government council: "(a) the formulation of economic planning and development schemes for the local government area; (b) collection of rates, radio and television licence fees; (c) establishment and maintenance of cemeteries, burial grounds and homes for the destitutes or infirm; (d) licensing of bicycles, trucks (other than mechanically propelled trucks), canoes, wheelbarrows and carts; (e) establishment and maintenance and regulation of slaughter-houses, slaughter slabs, markets, motor parks and public conveniences; (f) construction and maintenance of roads, streets, street lighting, drains, parks, gardens, open spaces, or such public facilities as may be prescribed from time to time by the House of Assembly of a State; (g) naming of roads and streets and numbering of houses; (h) provision and maintenance of public conveniences, sewage and refuse disposal; (i) registration of all births, deaths and marriages; (j) assessment of privately owned houses or tenements for the purpose of levying such rates as may be prescribed by the House of Assembly of a State; and (k) control and regulation of: (i) outdoor advertising and hoarding; (ii) movement and keeping of pets of all description; (iii) shops and kiosks; (iv) restaurants, bakeries and other places for sale of food to the public; (v) laundries; and (vi) licensing, regulation and control of the sale of liquor."

While these functions ought to be performed exclusively by the local governments, they are also expected to participate, along with the State Governments, in the following matters: "(a) the provision and maintenance of primary, adult and vocational education; (b) the development of agriculture and natural resources other than the exploitation of minerals; (c) the provision and maintenance of health services; and (d) such other functions as may be conferred upon a local government by the House of Assembly of the State."[18]

In brief, the functions exclusively entrusted to the local government fall under three categories, namely, provision of essential services, collection of local taxes which are generally prescribed by the State Government and a few attendant regulatory functions. The field of development activities is shared by the State and local governments, with the former playing a leading role, both in planning and in implementation. The involvement of local governments, much less the local people, in national planning is extremely insignificant at present, even though the 1989 Constitution does make it mandatory on the part of every local government to participate in the economic planning and development of the local area concerned and to this end a joint economic planning board has to be established by a law to be enacted by the House of Assembly of the State.[19]

Resources – Financial and Human

Before the 1976 national local government reforms which greatly improved the financial position of the local authorities, inadequacy of revenue was the most critical problem that constrained the development of local government in Nigeria. The main sources of local government finance then were: (1) the income or community tax; (2) fines and fees; (3) profits from trade and industry; (4) return on investments; and (5) grants, of which the first and the last only were significant.[20] At the time of the implementation of the reforms, the Federal Government committed to grant 10 per cent of its revenue whereas the State Governments would have to make grants at the level of five per cent of their revenues to the local governments. The exact allocation of the grants among the local governments, though based on equality, population and land area in most cases, however varied from State to State.

Unfortunately, neither the military regime nor the civilian government that came to power in 1979 kept up either the volume or the proportion of grants (though they could not entirely avoid making statutory grants to the local governments) and the endemic problem of inadequate finances continued to haunt the local governments. Learning from this experience, perhaps, the 1989 Constitution now specifically provides constitutional and legal guarantees for the allocation of revenue to the local government councils. Section 162(1) of the Constitution empowers the Federal Government to make grants-in-aid to local governments (currently 15 per cent). In addition, Section 160(4) of the Constitution now provides for the direct allocation of federal grants into the coffers of local governments rather than through the State Government as previously obtained. Further Section 123(3) empowers the auditor-general of the local governments of a State to audit the public accounts of a local government and of all offices of the local government. By Section 160(6), each State is required to pay local governments in its area of jurisdiction such proportion of the State's internally generated revenue as may be prescribed by the National Assembly (currently 10 per cent).

Though these steps will result in a significant rise in the total statutory allocations to the local governments which in turn will enhance the independence of local government councils in the execution of development works and improve their planning capabilities, there is also a possibility that it may result in some local governments and the State Governments abolishing or at least slackening the collection of some traditional sources of local government revenue, such as the community tax, etc.[21] In some areas the existing momentum for community self-help efforts may also dwindle. The resultant reduction in the internal revenue may increase the dependence of the local governments on the higher tiers for timely allocation of funds.

The Secretary to the local government is the head of the services of the local government, in charge of all its administrative management. He is the chief adviser to the local government council and to the finance and general purposes committee and coordinates the activities of all the departments of the local government.[22] He is a career civil servant belonging to the unified local government service. The organisational structure of a local government consists of (a) general administration department including personnel management; (b) department of finances, supplies, planning, research and statistics; (c) education; (d) agriculture and natural resources; (e) works, housing, land and survey; and (f) medical and health. No local government is allowed to have more than six departments in all.[23] Therefore, any expansion in the local government has to be accommodated through the subdivisions below the level of department provided that in each case the span of control does not exceed six. Each department is sub-divided into divisions to reflect broad professional areas within the department. Each division is sub-divided into branches to reflect sub-professional areas and each branch is sub-divided into sections to reflect specialised activities within a sub-professional area. In all cases the span of control shall not exceed six. The departments, divisions, branches and sections of a local government are all headed by an appropriate official of the local government service. In fact, an approved scheme of service for local government staff to make their cadre similar in terms and conditions to the State civil service has been drawn up to ensure that adequate local talent is attracted to the local government service.[24]

Each local government has a junior staff management committee headed by the secretary which will have the responsibility for the appointment, transfer, promotion and discipline of officers on grade levels 1-6. The appointment, transfer, promotion and discipline of senior officers who are in grade levels 7 and above will be the responsibility of the State Local Government Service Commission constituted for each State.[25] In fact, Section 200 of the 1989 Constitution clearly mentions that the State Local Government Service Commission shall not be subject to the direction or control of any other authority in exercising its powers to make appointments, or to exercise disciplinary control over these persons. The local government service commissions, as at present, are manned mostly by retired civil servants and academicians.

The Department of Local Government in each State contributes one per cent of its budget to training local government officers. Training needs are identified at local government levels and communicated to the Department which will then try to support the need. A proposal to link the local government service commission and the selection committee for training at the State level by appointing the chairman of the local government service commission as the chairman of the selection committee is under consideration, with a view to facilitating the human resource planning on the basis that the local government service commission knows the skill shortages at the local government level and this information could be used in selecting the personnel as well as the area for training.[26]

Conclusion

One significant factor that cannot be lost sight of in the Nigerian context is the increasing involvement of the Federal Government in local government affairs. Learning from the loopholes in the 1979 Constitution, which were exploited by the civilian politicians of the second republic, to weaken and demoralise the local government system, the subsequent 1989 Constitution clearly establishes the local government as a full-fledged third tier of the government with powers and functions of its own and has even gone to the extent of prescribing the mode of creating new local governments by the National Assembly in future. Increasing federal involvement, however, can have some adverse effects as well. Will uniformity in structure, powers and functions of the local governments across the country not threaten the very foundation of the concept of decentralisation, namely, that the local government should suit the local needs, traditions and aspirations of the people it serves? How will the civilian State Governments (as and when they come to power) react to the local government over which, they may feel, they have no adequate control?

As things stand now the system of local government by democratically elected local government councils has been guaranteed under the 1989 Constitution. The employees of the local government now enjoy conditions of service comparable with those of Federal and State Civil Services. Direct allocation of funds to the local government has also been made statutory. These developments have no doubt enhancd the status of the local government and with the establishment of elected local governments in December 1990, one should have hoped for a better performance from the local governments in Nigeria. Unfotunately, the return of complete political power to the elected representatives, which did take place during the second half of 1993, though not in the way it was originally intended, was short-lived and the country is back under military rule in November 1993. The new ruler, Gen. Abacha has, like most other military rulers, inaugurated his role with a lofty declaration that he desires to restore democracy in Nigeria. What this will mean, how long this will take and what will be its impact on local governments in Nigeria are questions that remain unanswered at least for the time being.

NOTES AND REFERENCES

1. This periodisation is based on the opening address of the secretary to the government of the Nigerian Federation, Alhaji Shehu Musa, at the international conference on the evolution of local governments in West Africa held at Ile-Ife, Nigeria, in February, 1982.
2. R. Wraith and M. Dent, *The British legacy of local self-government in West Africa revisited,* University of Lagos Press, 1988, p. 21.
3. Dele Olowu, *Developments in Anglophone West Africa*, University of Lagos Press, 1988, p. 294.
4. Local government review committee under the chairmanship of Alhaji Ibrahim Dasuki, 1984.
5. L. Adamolekun, D. Olowu and M. Laleye, *Local government in West Africa since independence*. University of Lagos Press 1988, p. 357.
6. *Guidelines for local government reform, 1976*. Government Printer, Kaduna, para 3.
7. *Ibid.*, para 1.
8. *The constitution of the federal republic of Nigeria, 1989*, section 7(1).
9. *Ibid.*, section 7(3).
10. *Guidelines for local government reform, 1976. op. cit.*, para 8.
11. Nigerian Constitution, *op. cit.*, section 9(3).
12. *Ibid.*, sections 284, 290, 291 and 298.
13. *Ibid.*, section 302.
14. *Ibid.*, sections 283 and 304.
15. Egwurube, J.O., *Traditional Rulers and Modern Local Government".* University of Lagos Press, 1988, p. 170.
16. *Guidelines for local government reform, 1976. op. cit.* para 21.
17. *Ibid.*, para 4.
18. Nigerian Constitution, 1989. *op.cit.* Fourth Schedule, Part 1 section 2 (p. 73)
19. *Ibid.*, section 7 (5).
20. Alex Gboyega, *Local government in Nigeria*, 1987, p. 165.
21. I.I. Ihinmodu, *Problems of revenue mobilisation in Kwara State: a case study of the effects of abolishing poll/community taxes.* University of Lagos Press, 1988.
22. Implementation guidelines on the application of civil service reforms in the local government service, Government Printer, Lagos, 1988. para 8.1.
23. *Ibid.*, para 11.2.
24. *Ibid.*, para 15.
25. *Ibid.*, para 12.4.
26. Ita O'Donovon, *Management and change in Northern Nigeria local government*, University of Birmingham, 1990.

3

CHINESE FORM OF LOCAL GOVERNMENTS

Situated in the northern half of the eastern hemisphere, the People's Republic of China lies in East Asia, on the west coast of the Pacific Ocean. As of now, it is the second largest country in the world, next only to Canada. It has a land area of approximately 9.6 million square kilometres, which makes it slightly larger than the United States of America, or about the size of Europe (excluding the erstwhile USSR). The Chinese mainland is flanked by the Bohai Sea, the Yellow Sea, the East China Sea and the South China Sea. Contiguous to each other, the four seas form a northeast-southwest arc covering a total area of 4.78 million square kilometres. China's land boundary exceeds 20,000 kilometres in length and is bordered by Korea in the northeast; Mongolia in the north; Afghanisthan, Pakisthan, Nepal, Bhutan and India in the southwest; and Burma, Laos and Vietnam in the south.The country is . divided into 23 provinces, five autonomous regions and three municipalities directly under the Central Government. With a population of 1.1 billion, which is unevenly distributed–the inland areas being relatively sparsely populated and coastal provinces densely populated-China is the most populated country in the world, supporting more than 22 per cent of the world's population on only 7 per cent of the world's areable land.[1]

History

As in the case of Nigeria the history of local government in China can also be divided into six major periods, each representing a significant era in her political history. These are: (a) the pre-1949 era, tha' is, until the People's Republic of China (PRC) came to be established; (b) the early period of Communism, that is, from 1949 to 1952 coinciding with the implementation of the land reforms law; (c) the era of collective farming (on the Soviet pattern) between 1952 and 1957; (d) the period of Maoism and the "cultural revolution" between 1958 and 1978; (e) the early period of "open policy" between 1978 and 1983, and (f) the second phase of political reforms since 1984.[2]

Prior to 1949 the Kuomintang China had a Bao-Jia system of local administration, a system organised on the basis of households. Each Jia was made up of 10 to 30 households; each Bao of 10 to 30 Jias and each district of 10 to 30 Baos. This system had been in vogue even during the days of imperial dynasties in most parts of China, though under different names. If the chief of each of these units was nominated by the Palace in the earlier days, they were chosen by the powerful landlords in the Kuomintang China. The functions they discharged were essentially the same, namely, to promote kinship among the citizens, collect taxes and duties and look after basic amenities. Their role was extremely minimal in the socio-economic development of the area, which, if any, was left to the will and pleasure of the ruler.

At the time of the proclamation of the PRC by Mao Zedong on October 1, 1949, the economy was at a standstill, communications almost wholly interrupted owing to the continuous civil war that preceded the proclamation, and public utilities run down by years of neglect. The new regime had to tackle these problems in right earnest besides chasing away the Kuomintang soldiers who tried to create sporadic problems, most notably in southern China. The implementation of land reforms with the specific objects of abolishing the feudal exploitative system of land ownership by the landlord class, introducing the system of peasant and land ownership in order to set free the rural productive forces, developing agricultural production and paving the way for China's new industrialisation, from the summer of 1950 to the spring of 1953, constituted the beginning of the construction of grassroot organs in China. Party organs were built up at the level of peasant associations which also functioned as government organs at that level.

However, it was during the period of collectivisation of farming that larger and larger groups of peasants with prominent leaders wielding considerable influence over the group came into prominence, and township units came to be established, consisting of one or more collectives depending upon their size. By 1957, there were over 100,000 townships in China to supervise which the federal government created over 10,000 public offices below the county level. Thus, agricultural production groups became the basic units of grassroot organs in the

PRC during this period.

Management of the cooperatives, however, demanded leadership and planning on a scale new to the countryside and in their absence a good deal of cadre inefficiency had emerged. In the situation of the mid-1950s Mao perceived a whole series of contradictions – between industry and agriculture, coast and interior, centre and localities, heavy industry and light industry, to quote a few – which needed to be resolved, if necessary, by an administered economy through a centralised bureaucracy. Mao, however, chose the option to decentralise mainly economic matters to local control, but keeping them within the centre's political sphere. In a decisive break with the previous strategy of planned and voluntary gradualism, almost the entire peasantry was organised into collectives in a single year. Two years later in the course of the "Great Leap Forward" these were further amalgamated into rural people's communes, which in due course became vehicles for a general re-organisation of rural life in preparation for a quick transition to communism.

By December 1958, virtually all 740,000 rural collectives containing over 120 million households had been reorganised into about 26,000 rural people's communes. The major difficulty facing the communes, however, was their enormous size. To overcome the problems of management and control, by 1961, efforts were made to reduce the size of the communes and by 1963, their number had gone up to 74,000, implying that the average commune was then only one-third of the original size. By the late 1970s the number had again been reduced to 50,000, possibly reflecting the gradual rural development, and membership per commune averaged 15,000.

From the beginning, the system had three tiers – the commune at the top, the production brigade (on an average about 9 to 13 brigades per commune) at the intermediate level, and the production team (averaging about 7 to 8 per brigade) at the bottom. The teams averaged 20 to 40 neighbouring households each. Since the collective used to be responsible for the distribution of income among its members originally, it was the commune that was initially made the unit of account in 1958, which later got shifted downwards first to the brigade and finally in 1962 to the team where, with some exceptions, it stayed for almost two decades.

The communes were multifunctional, responsible for local government, party affairs, social welfare (such as secondary education and hospitals), economic planning and management, culture, public security, rural investment projects, local industry and commerce, technical services, etc. The production brigade operated under the supervision of the commune and was responsible for political affairs, small-scale rural capital construction and industry and social welfare, such as elementary schools and clinics. The production team, often corresponding to the natural village, operated under the supervision of the brigade as the basic unit of agricultural production. The communes and their components were themselves subject to controls and claims exerted by the State, the lowest level of which above the commune was the county government. State controls operated through a dual system of both government and party organisations.

The commune itself acted as a dual institution – on the one hand it was a collective responsible to its component parts and members and, on the other, it was a representative of the State, in effect the basic level of local government and was, therefore, responsible to higher levels of the State. The commune and the brigades also had party organs which were subordinate to higher levels of the party apparatus. In consequence the autonomy of the communes, brigades and teams was heavily circumscribed and they were under heavy pressure to comply with the policies of the Party/State at any given time.[3]

Though the commune system performed reasonably well in terms of agricultural production, was able to establish a satisfactory system of rural health and educational facilities and also contributed to the diversification of rural economy by establishing rural industries and enterprises, it nevertheless concealed certain serious problems. While the egalitarian distribution practices kept the income differentials within bounds within the commune, they also dampened production incentives and thus hampered productivity growth. The inequality between the communes also persisted. The lack of autonomy in production – the teams were in fact told what to produce, whom to sell it to and at what price – resulted in a lack of commitment towards the full and better utilisation of the collective assets. Despite all these shortcomings, the commune system held its sway for almost 20 years in the PRC.

The need to stimulate agricultural growth finally led to the phase of decollectivisation in the post-Mao era, which started with the Third Plenum of the Eleventh Central Committee in December, 1978. The key points in the new economic programme then announced included reforming the commune system and decentralisation for both the local governments and the enterprises.[4]

The consequent introduction of the household responsibility system in agriculture virtually dismantled the system of people's communes in favour of a tripartite rural structure consisting of political, governmental and economic organs. Just as the commune system served to complement Mao's fusion theory of political economy by integrating government administration with commune management (*Zhengshe heyi*), the new political order was designed to serve the fission theory of Deng Xiaoping and the reformist leadership – separation of political and economic power, in order to promote rural entrepreneurship and efficient administration. To serve these ends, political reforms were introduced that called for reviving township governments and local elections, institutionalising division of responsibility among party, government and economic cadres, creating self-managing village committees and streamlining rural administration. The centre-piece of the reforms, namely, separating government administration from commune management (*Zhengshe fenkai*) by establishing town and township governments as the local organs of State power and creating separate and subordinate economic committees to replace the commune's collective economic functions was implemented between 1982 and 1985.

The history of local governments in China thus points out one underlying fact unmistakably, that is, political or structural reforms in China have been pursued primarily because of their contribution to rural economic development; their utility in service to political and social goals was only secondary.

Structure

According to the Constitution all power in PRC belongs to the people. This power is exercised through the People's Congresses at the different government levels up to and including the National People's Congress (NPC) at the apex. At present the control over State affairs in the PRC is, however, exercised by the Communist Party of China (CCP). In descending order of size these territorial and governmental levels are the nation, the province, the city, the municipality/county, the township/town and the natural village. While the deputies to the county and the township People's Congresses are directly elected by the people from a list of candidates drawn up by the election committee led by the local unit of the Party, deputies to the People's Congresses at higher levels are elected by the People's Congress at the next lower level. Their term of office is five years, while that of the directly elected deputies at levels below is three years.

Meetings of local People's Congresses are convened at least once a year and temporary meetings may be convened on the proposal of one-fifth of the deputies at the same level. When meetings are held, a Presidium is elected to preside over them and various necessary committees are established to carry out the work of the Congress under the leadership of the Presidium. And it is the Presidium which nominates, on its own, or jointly with the deputies of the respective Congresses, the administrative head of government at that level, that is, the provincial governor and deputy governors, the mayors and deputy mayors, the county heads and deputy heads and the town heads and deputy heads. The standing committees of the People's Congresses can make local statutes, but they can be implemented only with the approval of the People's Congress of the next higher level, and then reported to the National People's Congress Standing Committee and State Council for record. In addition, the Standing Committee calls sessions of the corresponding People's Congresses and acts on behalf of the People's Congress when it is not in session.

The State Council is the nation's supreme administrative organ. Having direct responsibility to the Central Government are the 23 provinces on the mainland, the five autonomous regions and the three special municipalities (the cities of Beijing, Shanghai and Tianjin).[5] These cities and some other large ones are sub-divided into districts which are the basic units of city government. These might comprise of both urban and rural areas and include 200 to 600 thousand people. The cities which are not sub-divided into districts, as well as the districts within municipalities, may set up sub-district offices which act as the agents of the city government for that area. If a county is large enough, it may also establish such sub-district offices.

The township/town is the lowest organ of the State power. (see Chart 1). By the end of 1989, China had 447 cities, 1,919 counties, 44,704 townships and 11,060 towns.[6]

The Neighbourhood Committees in the cities and the Village Committees in the rural areas are the basic mass organs which assist the respective local governments in matters of public affairs and public security. They are not units of government. The Neighbourhood Committees consisting of 10 to 15 members are responsible for family counselling and family planning, sanitation and street cleaning, child care services, care of the elderly, housing maintenance and repair, adjudication of family and inter-family disputes and programmes of assistance to youth. Their leaders are expected to act as an information network for the government in the urban neighbourhood, reporting on the needs and concerns of the local people.[7]

The Village Committees are the mass organisations representing the autonomy of villages at the grassroot levels, by way of self-management, self-education and self-service; they are responsible for handling the public affairs and utilities of the village, mediating disputes among villagers, assisting in maintaining public order and reporting villagers' opinions, demands and suggestions to the people's government.[8] Under the Village Committee Law, which went into trial implementation on June 1, 1988, a Village Committee consists of three to seven members (with at least one woman) and is elected by the Village Council to which it remains responsible. The township government is expected to offer guidance, support and assistance in the work of Village Committees, while the Village Committees should help their township in carrying out its work. The Village Committees should manage the land and other assets owned collectively by the villagers, according to the law, and teach them the rational utilisation of natural resources and protection and improvement of the ecological environment. The Village Council consists of all the villagers who are at least 18 years old. Each household may assign its representative to participate in the council. The Village Committee shall report its work to the council. Problems involving the interests of the entire village shall have to be submitted by the Village Committee to the Village Council for decision after discussion. The latter is also entrusted with the power to dismiss and elect new members of the Village Committee, as and when necessary.[9]

Functions and Powers

The functions and powers of the People's Congresses are laid down in the organic law of the local people's governments of the PRC. Basically, they are the same for all levels, although the scale and complexity vary in accordance with the size and importance of the respective units. In general, the responsibilities of the local government are: (a) to carry out the decisions of the State Council, the Local People's Congress and the People's Congresses at higher levels, the State Plan, the State Budget and any government policy in general; (b) to ensure mobilisation of local resources; (c) to carry out economic, sociocultural and public security tasks; (d) to maintain and protect State

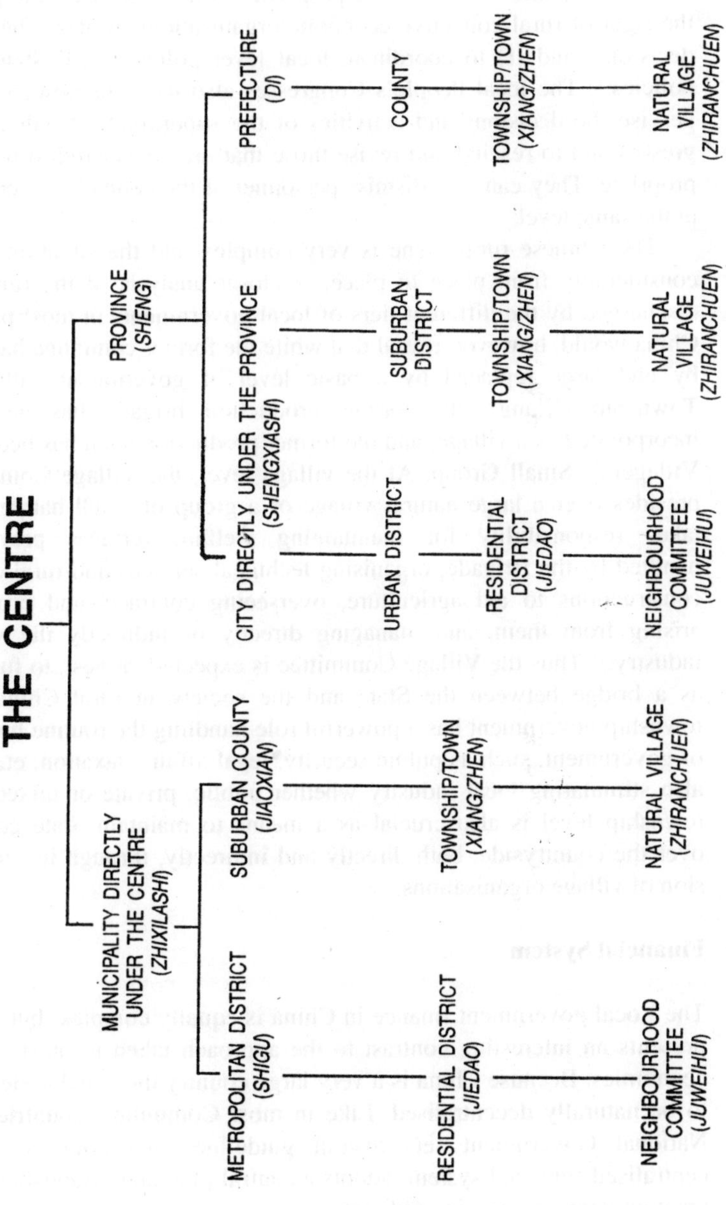
THE CENTRE
MUNICIPALITY DIRECTLY UNDER THE CENTRE (ZHIXILASHI)
PROVINCE (SHENG)
METROPOLITAN DISTRICT (SHIGU)
SUBURBAN COUNTY (JIAOXIAN)
CITY DIRECTLY UNDER THE PROVINCE (SHENGXIASHI)
PREFECTURE (DI)
RESIDENTIAL DISTRICT (JIEDAO)
TOWNSHIP/TOWN (XIANG/ZHEN)
URBAN DISTRICT
SUBURBAN DISTRICT
COUNTY
NEIGHBOURHOOD COMMITTEE (JUWEIHUI)
NATURAL VILLAGE (ZHIRANCHUEN)
RESIDENTIAL DISTRICT (JIEDAO)
TOWNSHIP/TOWN (XIANG/ZHEN)
TOWNSHIP/TOWN (XIANG/ZHEN)
NEIGHBOURHOOD COMMITTEE (JUWEIHUI)
NATURAL VILLAGE (ZHIRANCHUEN)
NATURAL VILLAGE (ZHIRANCHUEN)

owned companies as well as the properties of the citizens; (e) to protect the right of rural collective economic organisations to make their own decisions; and (f) to coordinate local level policies with State level policies.[10] The local People's Congresses also have the powers to supervise the decisions and activities of the subordinate People's Congresses and to rescind and revise those that are considered to be inappropriate. They can also dismiss personnel of the people's government at the same level.

The Chinese rural scene is very complex and the situation varies considerably from place to place. A closer analysis of the functions discharged by the different tiers of local governments in most parts of China would, however, reveal that while the former commune has been by and large replaced by a basic level of government called the Township (Xiang), the former production brigade has been reincorporated as a village, and the former production team has become a Villagers' Small Group. At the village level, the Village Committee presides over a large natural village or a group of small hamlets and takes responsibility for maintaining welfare services previously handled by the Brigade, organising technical services and rural capital constructions to aid agriculture, overseeing contracts and problems arising from them, and managing directly or indirectly the village industry.[11] Thus the Village Committee is expected, at best, to function as a bridge between the State and the society in rural China. The township government has a powerful role handling the routine business of government, such as public security, legal affairs, taxation, etc., and also stimulating local industry whether public, private or mixed. The township level is also crucial as a means to maintain State controls over the countryside, both directly and indirectly, through its supervision of village organisations.

Financial System

The Local government finance in China is equally complex, but it also presents an interesting contrast to the approach taken in most market economies. Because China is a very large country the fiscal system has to be naturally decentralised. Like in most Communist countries, the National Government sets overall guidelines and policies, has a centralised financial system, adopts a central plan and establishes local taxation items, categories and rates.

Taxes in China can be divided into four categories according to the disposition of their yield: (1) those of the Central Government, such as customs duties, sales and profit tax collections from centrally-owned enterprises; (2) those of the provincial governments, such as the taxes collected from provincial enterprises; (3) those shared among central, provincial and local governments, notably profit and sales taxes; and (4) those that are assigned exclusively to the local government. While the sales and profit taxes together usually account for 80 per cent or more of the local government revenues, there are other sources of local revenue also, such as animal slaughter tax, real estate tax, driving licence tax on vehicles and boats, domestic animal trade tax, taxes on service industries, etc. In addition, local government units are granted permission to levy a surcharge on national taxes on agricultural land, industrial and commercial activities, and urban public utilities for the improvement of these particular areas of activity.

Though local governments do receive occasional grants from the Central Government, as in most other countries, these are limited in amount and cannot cover all the needs, especially of units with little sources of own income. In actual practise, the financial resources available to local governments in the PRC are largely determined, firstly, by the number of taxes they levy and, secondly but more importantly, by the number of enterprises and undertakings they control. These range from all types of manufacturing – from screws to cast iron; from electronic equipment and various household products to agricultural products, such as canned fruits, vegetables, cotton, etc.

In respect of the common set of taxes shared by the central, provincial and local governments, policy decisions are made by the Central Government, but the tax assessment and collection is left to the local governments. The structure of shared taxes gives local governments substantial inducements to adjust their taxing and spending behaviour, but it also gives them access to productive tax bases.

Local governments in China have little independence in matters of structuring their own tax system, and are constrained by higher-level mandates in deciding on the level and composition of expenditure. All tax rates, and bases are set centrally, hence provincial and local taxes in China can be described as Central Government taxes whose revenues are allocated fully or partially to provinces, cities and counties. This does not mean that local governments have no impact on spending or revenues; in fact, provincial governments have the responsibility to design and implement a system of provincial and local sharing and local governments are responsible for tax administration.[12]

Moreover, both levels influence the operations of their enterprises. Provincial governments can alter the tax-sharing arrangements for each city/county within the province, give grants in any way they choose, and are responsible for approving the budgets and financial plans of these local governments. Because they set the tax-sharing rates, they may also indirectly affect the local government tax collection. The local governments control tax collection and assessment with what appears to be a minimum of direct central or provincial supervision. This responsibility puts a very powerful policy instrument in the hands of the local government and there is evidence that they use it.

The fiscal autonomy in China has a direct impact on the growth of the tax base as well. For example, the township governments can increase the production quotas of the enterprises, or can form new enterprises. They can also take administrative and fiscal actions to improve their efficiency and profitability. This local fiscal autonomy thus highlights a fundamental difference between the role of local governments in China and in market economies. In most Western countries local governments have substantial control over the tax rate, but virtually no control over the growth in the tax base. Local governments in China are in somewhat the reverse position. They have little say in the tax rate determination, but can have a substantial direct effect on the growth of local enterprises.

The second major difference is in the mode of tax sharing. As mentioned above, China's revenue sharing system is primarily a division of sales and profit taxes among the central, provincial and local governments. Whereas in most countries the taxes are collected by the Central Government and then allocated to the local governments, in China they are collected by the local governments and shared up to the higher levels. The Central Government determines a specified share of all taxes collected in each province to be passed on to it. In theory, the share is fixed for a period of years and is generally meant to reflect the difference between fiscal capacity and expenditure needs. The variation across provinces is, however, wide, from Shanghai's retention rate of about one-fourth of tax collections to several provinces which are allowed to retain all collections and also receive an additional payment from the Centre.

An important dimension of inter-governmental relations is the degree to which the provincial government redistributes taxable capacity, for instance, from rich to poor counties or from urban to rural areas. The most powerful fiscal tool which the province can use is that it may vary the tax-sharing ratios for each local government, apparently without any Central Government approval, and on an *ad hoc* basis.

Local governments in China cannot run a deficit and cannot borrow. There is no regular grant programme to support capital projects or current expenditures. There is no mechanism or formal programme for lending to local governments and there are no guidelines for local governments to develop beneficiary financing schemes. However, the local government owned enterprises can borrow, and in some cases the local governments have pledged their general revenues to secure the loans.[13]

From the revenue earned, many local government units maintain and expand the home production units and industries, as well as develop the local, cultural, educational, public health, scientific and other facilities and amenities. However, the scope of local financial activities is established at the national level and the expenditure quotas for the various fields of activities are handed down from the Central Government to the field agencies. While the local governments have no power to change the overall amounts for the various activities, they are, however, allowed to make adjustments between the line items.

While the fiscal system in China has some very great strengths as regards local government financing, it has its share of problems, especially in the areas of revenue adequacy and growth, the tax structure and tax-sharing system and the tax administration.[14] As is the case with most countries Chinese local governments are also starved of revenue. A combination of a backlog in the infrastructure needs and increasing urbanisation has put a great pressure on the local budgets. Further, the overall elasticity of the profit and sales taxes is also relatively low; in fact there is even a proposal now to levy property tax on rural households to augment the local government resources.

The Chinese system of taxation and tax sharing includes a number of penalties and incentives that sometimes have an adverse effect on the enterprises and the local governments. For instance, a low tax sharing ratio may reduce the incentive of the local government to efficiently collect taxes. The absence of borrowing and self-financing mechanisms creates a bias against infrastructure investments, because the full cost is shifted on to the general public and to current beneficiaries. The very high rate of taxation of profits provides a disincentive for local managers to maximise profitability. Worse it gives an incentive for extravagant expenditure and evasion and avoidance to the enterprise and perhaps to the local government that owns it.

The tax administration system is very complicated and, therefore, not easily administered. There are three different sales taxes levied on different types of sales at more than 60 different rates. The profits tax has three different rate schedules, includes six different taxes on profits and the use of profits and provides special treatment for certain enterprises. Record-keeping is also a problem. While the small firms do not keep any books of account, the books maintained by larger enterprises are often found to be inadequate. Finally, the size and competence of the local government staff to administer the system also leaves much to be desired. Despite all these shortcomings, the Chinese local governments do not suffer from any liquidity problems primarily because of their tax base (including the number of enterprises they control) and the system of tax sharing which puts the local government at an advantageous position, as against the higher tiers.

Structural Reform

While discussing the human resource availability to the decentralised organs of State power in China, one has to bear in mind the historical fact that in China, it is the basic party unit that has to plan and execute any rural project and the administrative structure at the decentralised levels has been traditionally weak. However, a direct consequence of the "decollectivisation" and the household responsibility system in 1978 was the obvious reduction in authority of the rural party/government cadres over the production processes. The commune structural reform that followed came to them as a second blow in as much as they faced a direct threat to their jobs, besides authority and prestige, this time. To keep their morale up the centre had to move cautiously, by creating suitable new organs of rural power. That explains why the organisational changes that were implemented between 1982 and 1985 in the PRC resulted in significant increases nationwide in the number of commune level (township and town) units.

The revival of township governments and the creation of separate and subordinate economic committees did not really make any significant departure, in actual practice. Most of the commune cadres got rehabilitated, either in the township government or in its economic committee. In fact, there were allegations in some provinces that, there had been little change in the style and methods of work and in reality there were three signposts, but only one boss – the local party secretary. A number of case studies have revealed that the commune structural reform did not result in the desired horizontal division of powers and that in some localities the party committee continued to act as local government. Even now a number of township heads and economic committee directors serve concurrently as deputy party secretaries; deputy township heads remain party committee members; and party committees assign responsibility for local government and economic work to individual secretaries.[15]

In addition to separation of government administration, the economic management and the party, the new reforms also aimed at streamlining administration, reducing the number of grassroot cadres and promoting younger and better educated persons to cadre posts. These changes were to serve three purposes. First, the rural economy could be liberated from the bureaucratic structure, granting more decision-making authority to individuals, groups and villages. Second, the direct financial burden of peasant households to support local administration could be reduced. Third, the promotion of younger and more qualified persons to leadership posts could improve grassroot economic management and facilitate a more rapid acceptance of the new work methods and relationships implied by the structural reform.

The extent to which these goals are met is not entirely clear. But, available information suggests a mixed result. Between 1983 and 1985 a number of scattered reports indicated that specific localities had reduced the number of cadres and promoted younger and more qualified persons as a result of the reform.[16] But, at least one report noted that the number of township cadres was increasing. Taken together the reports suggest that while the number of cadres at the village level and below has been significantly reduced, the number of township level personnel has actually grown as a result of the reforms. That impression is confirmed by the reported results of a survey conducted by the Rural Policy Research Centre of the party secretariat, and the Rural Development Research Centre of the State Council.

Human Resources

Assessing the availability and competence of personnel to serve the local government cadres in China is extremely difficult as the situation varies from province to province. If information publicly available on the party at the national level is scarce, much more so it is on the basic units. The separation of the administration from the economic management requires separation of government from party which bound together both the administration and the management of the economy under the erstwhile commune system. The authoritative guidelines issued in 1987 indicate that local party committees at the provincial, city and county levels must exercise political leadership over local work. Their main responsibilities are to implement the directives from the CCP central committee and from higher party and government organisations in the local area, to propose policy decisions on important local problems, to recommend outstanding cadres to local State organs and to coordinate the activities of various local organisations. The relationship between the local party committees and the corresponding government organs was to be evolved through practice and gradually form a regular system. Though, in theory, the party is to confine itself to reviewing the annual plan, formulate changes if necessary, draw up plans for city construction, drought relief and afforestation and forward them to the administration for implementation, in practise, however, the line between the party and the government, or between policy formulation and monitoring of its implementation at the local level usually gets blurred.

At the basic level of administration, i.e. at the township, apart from the heads of administration who are appointed by the local People's Congress, the administrative cadres comprise those who are sent down from the county administration and those whom the township administration directly appoints. Under the direction of the county administration, the township administration has started introducing the practise of public examination and selection by public invitation. Cadre allocation below the provincial level is decided at the provincial level and invariably the administrative cadres to be sent to the rural areas are determined at the county level. Currently, at the township level there are more than 20 branches of the county administration. The familiar phenomenon in local administration, viz. the responsibility of officials vertically to their higher organs and horizontally to the local superiors, has drawn critical comments at the local level. Added to them are the complaints that the officials sent from the county level are too many and often lack awareness of local conditions.

In the context of local administration an interesting experiment held as a model is reported from Huaxun county in Guilin province,[17] where administrative responsibility over its cadres has been handed down to a township under an agreement covering personnel, property and materials; the terms of the agreement are that (a) the township administration will not change the job classification, status, salary and welfare benefits of the officials nor the State planned allocation of finance and materials; (b) subject to the formal approval of the county administration, the township administration will have the power to dismiss the officials if necessary; (c) such powers over party cadres in the administration will be exercised by the party branch at the township level; and (d) in any transfer, promotion or removal from office of the officials at the township level, the county administration has to seek the concurrence of the township administration. Such models are still exploratory in nature and are yet to take root in the system.

The retirement age of the administrative cadres has been fixed at 60 years for males and 55 for females with a minimum of 15 years of service. In the party, for cadres holding senior positions at the Centre, and in provinces, cities and autonomous regions the retirement age is 65. Subject to the approval of higher authorities the cadres can leave the administration or the party. To encourage a younger age composition and the exit of cadres of the Cultural Revolution vintage, a series of incentives have also been announced. According to one estimate, of the total 5.97 million staff and workers in China, 1.43 million are working at the county level and below. Of the leading cadres 0.4 million operate from the county level and below out of a total of 1.4 million.[18]

To summarise, the dual hierarchy in China runs through the entire local government system, with the administrative and party machinery overlapping each other. However, as a result of the reforms, better progress has been achieved on the goal of promoting younger and better educated cadres than either in the horizontal division of powers or in reducing the number of rural cadres. The strength of the administrative establishment looks impressive, but their capacity to keep the administration distinct from the party needs to be established.

Conclusion

Though China's governmental system is more unitary than federal, they do have three distinct levels of government – central, provincial and local. While the county and the township form the key levels of the local government sector, the Village Committees are only mass organisations for self-management at the grassroot level. Under the principles of a Socialist State, in which leadership is exercised by the Communist Party, all levels of administration are part of a unified whole.

with the people's congresses, standing committees and administrative heads responsible to the party organs at the same level as well as to their counterparts at the higher levels of government. Thus, statutes and decisions taken at any level are subject to review by the higher levels and to revision or annulment, if considered inappropriate. The appointment and removal of administrative heads and other key officials also have to be approved by the next higher level.

The Constitution of the PRC makes it clear that "the local people's governments at various levels are responsible to the State administrative organs at the next higher level and make reports to them. The local people's governments at all levels throughout the country are organs of State administration under the unified leadership of the State Council, and are subordinate to the State Council."[19] Under these circumstances, what is obtaining in the PRC cannot really be classified as decentralisation. Though the lower tiers have certain freedom in implementation, even that is subject to the strict supervision of the local party organ, which again is vertically controlled. Hence it can at best be said that the local government system in the PRC is an effort at administrative deconcentration to achieve a possible economic development by an unitary Central Government. The creation of the Village Committees as units of self-management is, however, a step in the right direction, which may well become the forerunner for many more changes in the system of governance in the PRC.

NOTES AND REFERENCES

1. Qi Wen, *China–A general survey*. Foreign Languages Press, Beijing, 1989.
2. The periodisation and the historical details are based on my discussions with Mr. Wang Zhen Yao, chief of countryside division, department of grassroots organs of State power, Ministry of Civil Affairs, PRC.
3. Gordon White, *State Socialist Economic Reform and Rural Development: The Chinese Experience of Decollectivisation*, IDS, Sussex, 1991.
4. Deng Xiaoping, Selected works of Den Xiaoping (1974-82), Foreign Languages Press, Beijing, 1984.
5. Qi Wen, *op. cit.* In the official publications of PRC, Taiwan is also shown as one among the 23 provinces in PRC.
6. *China statistical year book*, 1990.
7. Eileen Martin Harloff/Cuiyi Wei, *Present Day Local Government in China*. Planning and Administration. 1989-2
8. The organic law governing Village Committees of the PRC (trial) adopted by the 23rd meeting of the 6th NPC standing committee on 24-11-1987. Article 2.

9. *Ibid.*, Article 11.
10. Eileen Martin Harloff/Cuiyi Wei, *op. cit.*
11. Gordon White, *op. cit.*
12. Roy Bahl, *World Development Report, 1988.* World Bank.
13. *Ibid.*
14. *Ibid.*
15. This observation is based on my field visits to a number of townships in Laixi county, Shandong Province.
16. See *Xinhua*, The New China News Agency, 29-3-1983.
17. Thiagarajan Manoharan, "Basic party units and decentralised development", *Copenhagen Papers*, Centre for East and Southeast Asian Studies, Museum Tuseulanum Press, 1990.
18. *Ibid.*
19. Constitution of the PRC, 1982. Article 112.

4

PANCHAYATI RAJ IN INDIA

India, the seventh largest country in the world by area and the second largest by population, covers an area of 3.29 million square kilometres, with about 15,200 kilometres long land frontier and a coast-line of about 6,100 kilometres. Her northern boundary is demarcated by the Himalayas and other mountain ranges, except in the Nepal region, which is marked by low hills. China, Bangladesh, Nepal and Bhutan are her neighbours in the north-east, Pakisthan and Afghanisthan in the north-west and Myanmar in the east. Below the broad territorial expanse of northern India is peninsular India, with the Arabian Sea to its west, the Bay of Bengal on the east and the Indian Ocean on the south.

India's 25 States and 7 Union Territories have a population of about 846 million (census 1991 figures), with an average density of population per square kilometre at 257. India got her independence from the British rule on August 15, 1947, and is now a soverign democratic socialist secular republic, which has a written Constitution that came into force on January 26, 1950.

History

Village communities common to most agrarian economies have been in existence in India for over centuries. They were called "Panchayats" – councils of five persons, one in every village. Jawaharlal Nehru points out in *The Discovery of India* that in olden days "the Village Panchayat or elected council had large powers both executive and judicial and its members were treated with the greatest of respect by the King's officers. Lands were distributed by this Panchayat which also collected taxes out of the produce and paid the government's share on behalf of the village. Over a number of these village councils there was a larger Panchayat or council to supervise and interfere if necessary".[1] Sir Charles Metcalfe, a British Governor in India during the 19th century, called them "little republics having nearly everything they want within themselves and almost independent of foreign relations. They seem to last where nothing else lasts".[2]

Under the British rule in India the autonomy of the Panchayats gradually disappeared owing to the establishment of local civil and criminal courts, revenue and police organisations, the increase in communications, the growth of individualism and operation of the individual *Ryotwari* (landholder-wise) System.[3] The British, however, attempted to establish an alternative system of local self-government in India. Lord Ripon, a British Viceroy, took the policy initiative in 1882 of establishing popularly elected institutions, at local levels, presided over by non-official chairmen to look after specified functions delegated to them by the provincial governments in their areas. Thereafter, village panchayats, district boards, town municipalities and city corporations came into existence in different parts of the country. These institutions, however, lacked in resources as well as autonomy. In addition, the caste-ridden feudal structure had an overriding influence on these local bodies.

It was Gandhiji who, for the first time in the 20th century, wished to revive the Panchayats with democratic bases of their own and invest them with adequate powers so that the villagers could have a real sense of "Swaraj", or self-rule. Gandhiji's idea of *village swaraj* was that the village would be "a complete republic independent of its neighbours for its own vital wants and yet inter-dependent for many others in which dependence is a necessity. The government of the village will be conducted by the Panchayat of five persons annually elected by the adult villagers, male and female, possessing minimum prescribed qualifications. These will have all the authority and jurisdiction required. Since there will be no system of punishment in the accepted sense, the Panchayat will be the legislature, judiciary and executive combined to operate for its year of office. Here there is perfect democracy based upon individual freedom. The individual is the architect of his own government."[4]

Unfortunately, these views of the Father of the Nation had not been shared by many, most notably by Dr. Ambedkar – the legal luminary whose contribution to the drafting of the Indian Constitution has been the most significant – who in the Constituent Assembly said, "what is the village, but a sink of localism, a den of ignorance, narrow-mindedness and communalism?".[5] He believed that these village republics have been the ruination of India. The condition of the caste-ridden Indian village at that time was such that one can easily understand why Dr. Ambedkar thought this way. His strong opposition to the concept of village as the basic unit of administration had resulted in the Panchayats not even finding a mention in the first draft of independent India's Constitution. While Gandhiji considered it as "an omission calling for immediate attention if our independence is to reflect the people's voice",[6] some others felt that "Dr. Ambedkar's attitude was typical of the urban high-brow"[7] and that "without the foundation stone of village Panchayats in our country how would it be possible for our masses to play their rightful part in our democracy"?[8]

These criticisms persuaded the president of the Constituent Assembly to write to the constitutional adviser, asking him whether the whole thing could be re-examined and the Constitution re-drafted from that point of view. But, it was then too late in the process of constitution making to re-draft the whole Constitution having the Panchayats as its base. It was, therefore, thought better to incorporate the Panchayats in the Directive Principles of State Policy and retain the framework of parliamentary government based on direct popular elections both at the Centre and in the States of the Indian Union. Article 40 of the Constitution merely states that "the State shall take steps to organise village Panchayats and endow them with such powers and authority as may be necessary to enable them to function as units of self-government". This left little obligation to implement Panchayati Raj (or the system of rural local governments) in independent India. There was no legislation to implement it until 1959. Finally, it came about when India realised that it was impossible to implement the development programmes without the instrument of people's participation.

The advent of national planning in India during the fifties broadened the scope of rural extension. The First Five Year Plan visualised Panchayats at the village level mainly as agencies for development, public welfare and land reforms. It wished that the Panchayats at the village level were so organised as to enable them to assume the agency functions of the higher authorities.[9] The Second Five-Year Plan went a step further and specifically recommended a network of active Panchayats for securing (a) comprehensive village planning; (b) a more just and integrated social structure in rural areas; (c) development of a new type of leadership in order to facilitate the process of rapid transition of the rural society; and (d) a complete pattern of development administration in the districts envisaged in the programmes of community development and national extension services".[10]

With the inauguration of the community development programme in October 1952, the blocks (consisting of about 150 to 200 villages) had become units of development administration within the existing districts. Those at the helm of affairs realised that without an agency at the village level, which could represent the entire community, assume responsibility and provide the necessary leadership for implementing development programmes, real progress in rural development could not come about.[11] This led to the appointment of a team for the study of Community Projects and National Extension Services headed by Shri Balwantrai G. Mehta in January 1957.

The team was expected to review the economy and efficiency of community development projects and national extension services and assess the extent to which the movement had succeeded in utilising local initiative and creating institutions to ensure continuity in the process of improving economic and social conditions in rural areas. The recommendations of the Balwantrai Mehta study team signalled the beginning of Panchayati Raj in independent India.

The study team said: "Admittedly one of the least successful aspects of community development and national extension service work is its attempt to evoke popular initiative. So long as we do not discover or create a representative and democratic institution which will supply the local interest, supervision and care necessary to ensure that expenditure of money upon local objects conforms with the needs and wishes of the locality, invest it with adequate power and assign to it appropriate finances, we will never be able to evoke local interest and excite local initiative in the field of development".[12] Therefore, it recommended the establishment of a three-tier Panchayati Raj, the middle tier, namely, the Panchayat Samiti at the block level playing the pivotal role in the scheme of decentralisation. The Samiti's jurisdiction was to be coterminous with that of the community development block, the members being directly elected.

The elected chairmen of the Panchayat Samitis together with the members of the State Legislature and of the Parliament representing a part or whole of the district and key officers of the development departments at the district level would constitute the Zilla Parishad (ZP) for the district with the District Collector/Deputy Commissioner as the Chairman. The ZP was visualised essentially as an advisory body. The village or Gram Panchayat would constitute the lowest level in the three-tier structure. Each level of this structure would have the power to require the lower level to function as its agent. The budget of the Village Panchayat was to be approved by the Panchayat Samiti and that of the Samiti by the ZP.

The recommendations of the Balwantrai Mehta study team were considered by the National Development Council (NDC), the highest forum, representing the Central Government and the State Governments in regard to matters of planning in India's federal system, in January, 1958. The NDC endorsed the basic principle of democratic decentralisation as formulated by the study team and asked the State Governments to devise their own Panchayat systems which would suit their local conditions. By 1959 all the States had passed their (Panchayat) Acts and by the mid-1960s Panchayats had reached all parts of the country. Over 217,300 Village Panchayats covering over 96 per cent of about 579,000 inhabited villages and 92 per cent of the rural population came into existence under about 4,500 Panchayat Samitis and about 330 ZPs (of different nomenclatures, however, to suit the local languages).[13] On an average a Panchayat covered a population of about 2,400 and a Samiti about 48 Panchayats.

Though there were variations from State to State, broadly the functions entrusted to the Panchayats included village roads, community wells, maintenance of public parks, tanks, irrigation works, public hygiene, drainage, and other civic services. In some States the ZPs were made responsible for primary education and were entrusted with functions relating to rural industries, primary health care, medical relief, women and child welfare, maintenance of common grazing grounds and other community lands and properties and provision of inputs for agricultural production. The extent and tempo of the involvement of the Panchayati Raj institutions (PRIs) in the basic planning and implementation of development projects was also subject to wide variations from State to State and even within the States. A report of the Ministry of Community Development had said in 1964-65 that younger and better leadership was emerging through the PRIs and there was a fairly high degree of satisfaction among the people with the working of the PRIs.[14] Admittedly, the PRIs gave a boost to the emergence of local leadership by creating new seats of power to be filled by the competitive mechanism of democratic elections.

This phase of ascendancy in the history of the Panchayati Raj in India continued till 1964, to be followed by a phase of stagnation (1965-69) and then a phase of decline (1969-1977).[15] With the passing away of the first Prime Minister of India, Pandit Jawaharlal Nehru, the commitment to democratic values weakened. The flow of funds for block development slowed down to a trickle, after the closure of the intensive stages of the Community Development Programme. Where the party in power apprehended that their performance in the polls to the PRIs may not be good, the tendency was to postpone elections indefinitely. The decline was conspicuous in every State except Maharashtra and Gujarat, where the primacy was with the top tier, namely, the ZPs, which had considerable administrative powers. Even in these States, Ministers and Members of Legislative Assembly (MLAs) felt threatened by the rising political power and influence of the ZP presidents and there was a kind of backlash. The Government of Maharashtra, for instance, set up separate district planning committees with the State minister in charge of that district as chairman; the planning responsibility which was one of the major functions of the ZP was taken over by this committee and the stature of the ZP was deliberately curtailed. The same situation occurred in Gujarat also almost simultaneously.

Several causes contributed to the decline of the PRIs. Firstly, the bureaucracy, local vested interests and the elected representatives in the State Legislature and in the Parliament did not take kindly to the PRIs, whose ascendancy they feared. In 1966-67 the Ministry of Community Development was reduced to the status of a department and brought under the Ministry of Food and Agriculture. In 1971 the very name "Community Development" was dropped and replaced by "Rural Development".

Secondly, the political leadership, planners and bureaucracy considered the PRIs mostly as agencies of development and not as little republics. This was a serious conceptual flaw. While the rationale for the creation of the PRIs was that "development cannot progress without responsibility and power", the thrust in the five-year plans had been to establish statutory Panchayats more as vehicles for National Extension and Community Development projects than as units of self-government, with the result the PRIs had no autonomy and were under the mercy of the State Governments and their bureaucracy.

Thirdly, there was a strong tendency in India, as in many other parts of the world, to concentrate power at the centre to an excessive degree and hand over "the levers of power in the hands of an elite which manages private industry and trade through giant commercial companies, runs nationalised industries through public corporation and public administration through a civil service working in the shadow of the ministers whose powers they exercise".[16] Even the Ford Foundation team of experts while enquiring into India's acute food shortage came to the conclusion that local autonomy would be a luxury in India's case and recommended for a single line of command and obedience.[17] The net result of all this was the creation of parallel agencies to execute special development programmes such as the Small Farmers Development Agency, Drought Prone Area Programme, Intensive Tribal Development Project, etc., which were kept outside the purview of the PRIs, which in turn resulted in further weakening of these nascent institutions.

Fourthly, most of the State Governments would not hold elections to the PRIs for years together, under one pretext or the other. Elected chairmen were suspended or removed in many cases; and some PRIs were superseded on flimsy political considerations. There was also the phenomenon of the tapering-off of resources to these bodies, both by the Central and State Governments. This lack of political will hastened the decline of the PRIs.

Fifthly, there was also a feeling that the PRIs are dominated by economically or socially privileged sections of society and have as such facilitated the emergence of oligarchic forces yielding no benefits to weaker sections. Even though the PRIs cannot be singled out in this connection, a number of research studies have in fact indicated that development benefits through these institutions had gone largely to the economically well-off, socially high-ups, in stratification, and politically advantaged sections of the rural communities; and the weaker sections were either deprived in the process or marginally benefited.[18]

And, finally, it must be admitted that notwithstanding the unwillingness of the State-level politicians to part with their power, even the people themselves were not sufficiently educated to understand the political implications of the PRIs. If the challenge from the grassroot level was effective, probably the PRIs would have put up a better show.

While the democratically elected PRIs were undergoing a decline, the North Eastern States of India, especially the hill areas such as the Nokmas of Garo Hills, the Syiems and Sirdars of Khasi Hills and the Dolois of Jaintia Hills which inherited their own system of grassroot, indigenous, democratic institutions continued with their own version of the Panchayati Raj, based on their tribal culture wherein the village elders used to nominate the members of the Panchayat in such a way that all the clans got their due representation.

The revival of interest in the Panchayati Raj came about with a change of government at the national level during 1977. A committee was then set up under the chairmanship of Shri Ashok Mehta to take a fresh look at the whole situation. This committee re-emphasised the importance of Panchayati Raj, but recommended a two-tier structure – ZP at the district level and Mandal Panchayat (MP) for a group of villages, with a population of 20,000-30,000 (i.e. below the block level), the key level being the ZP. It also recommended that the district should be the first point for decentralisation under popular supervision below the State level and favoured the official recognition of the participation of political parties at all levels of Panchayat elections.[19]

Though the Morarji Desai Government at the centre went out of office before any action could be considered on the Ashok Mehta Committee recommendations and most of the States, continued rather reluctantly with some version or the other of the three-tier system of local government recommended by the Balwantrai Mehta study team, three States – West Bengal, Karnataka and Andhra Pradesh – have nevertheless tried, since then, to put into practice the recommendations of the Ashok Mehta Committee with changes and modifications suitable to their tradition and context.

Any study on democratic decentralisation in India will, therefore, have to essentially cover at least three models – the time-tested Maharashtra and Gujarat model which has been in operation ever since the acceptance of the recommendation of the Balwantrai Mehta study team; the West Bengal model which was the first to undergo a change after the submission of the Ashok Mehta Committee report; and the subsequent Karnataka model. (The Andhra Pradesh model has certain features in common with each of these models.) The first, to many observers, has undergone, in recent years, a perceptible decline; the second is stable and the third which came into operation in 1987 was easily the most progressive. While a detailed study of the Karnataka model is, therefore, essential to know the latest thinking on the subject, a good knowledge of the other two models would also be necessary to facilitate such a study. We shall, therefore, take a quick look at the basic features of the first two models in this chapter and then take up the Karnataka model for a fairly detailed study, contrasting it with the Andhra Pradesh system in the next chapter. All these models will, however, be undergoing some changes during 1994, so as to bring them in conformity with the mandatory provisions of the Constitution (Seventy third Amendment) Act, 1992, which has been brought into force with effect from April 24, 1993.

The Maharashtra-Gujarat Model

When the Balwantrai Mehta study team submitted its report in November 1957, the then composite Bombay State was engaged in evolving a common Village Panchayat system for the entire State. Accepting the recommendations of the study team on the establishment of the PRIs in principle, the Government of Bombay decided to undertake legislation in this behalf only after the base was ready, i.e. when a uniform pattern of Village Panchayats throughout the State was established. With this end in view, a comprehensive legislation in respect of Village Panchayats, namely, the Bombay Village Panchayats Act, was enacted in 1958. Meanwhile the composite Bombay State was bifurcated and it was, therefore, left to the new States of Maharashtra and Gujarat to work out their own systems of the three-tier Panchayati Raj.

Immediately after the inauguration of the Maharashtra State on May 1, 1960, the Government of Maharashtra set up a committee under the Chairmanship of Shri V.P. Naik, the then Revenue Minister, to study the recommendations of the Balwantrai Mehta Committee and to suggest ways for its efficient implementation in the State. The Committee came to the conclusion that "considering the various aspects, we think that it should be possible to establish democratic bodies, invest them with the necessary authority and provide them with suitable administrative machinery and financial resources, so that they would be able to plan and implement all schemes of a local nature with efficiency, speed and economy. The fundamental purpose of decentralisation should be to train the local leadership to assume higher responsibilities and to serve the people with maximum efficiency and economy."[20] Following the enactment of the Panchayat Samiti and Zilla Parishads Act, 1961, Panchayati Raj in Maharashtra was inaugurated on May 1, 1962.

Following a similar pattern, the three-tier Panchayat structure under the Gujarat Panchayats Act, 1961 (which was based on the recommendations of the Democratic Decentralisation Committee, constituted by the Government of Gujarat and headed by the then Home Minister of Gujarat, Shri Rasiklal Parikh), took office in Gujarat on April 1, 1963.

The Maharashtra Act provided for a three-tier system with the top tier, namely, the ZP, as the key level of decentralisation. The ZP has a minimum of 40 and a maximum of 60 councillors directly elected by the people. There is also a provision for coopting representatives of cooperative societies in addition to members from the Scheduled Castes (SCs), Scheduled Tribes (STs) and women. For the convenience of its day-to-day working the ZP is divided into several subject committees, namely, Standing Committee, Finance Committee, Agricultural and Animal Husbandry Committee, Works Committee, Health Committee, Social Welfare Committee and Education Committee.The ZP elects a President, vice-president and the Chairmen of the Subject Committees from amongst its members. A member can hold the office of president or vice-president for a maximum of two terms (that is, 12 years) only. Other than through a no-confidence motion, the President or a Vice-President can be removed from office by the State Government also for negligence of duty or misconduct; and the President or Vice-President so removed shall not be eligible for re-election as president or vice-president during the remaining period of the term of his office.

The ZP has been entrusted with full executive authority with respect to development functions which were earlier discharged by the State Government at the district level. The ZPs have also been entrusted with some responsibilities in the sphere of revenue collection. The District Collector has been kept outside the ZP and another officer equal to the rank of the collector has been given to the ZP so that developmental activities may receive adequate attention. It was argued that the Collector is already overburdened and overworked and cannot be saddled with further work. The suggestion of the Naik Committee, namely, that by keeping the Collector outside the local body, the government will have in him an independent officer who can also evaluate impartially the functioning of the local body and can keep the government informed on any matter which is of sufficient importance, was agreed to and the Collector was invested with certain controlling powers which he already enjoyed in regard to the then existing local bodies.

Administrative leadership of the ZP rests with the Chief Executive Officer. Generally he belongs to the State cadre of the Indian Administrative Service and he is appointed by the State Government. He exercises all the powers specifically vested in him. He attends the meetings of the ZP and all its committees. He can call for any information, returns, statement, account or report from any officer of the ZP. He appoints Class III and IV officials (the junior cadres) and grants leave for a particular period to Class I and Class II officers. If two-thirds of the total number of ZP members so request, he has to be withdrawn from that ZP by the State Government.

The middle tier, namely, the Panchayat Samiti (at the block level), consists of elected, nominated and coopted members. It functions as a link between the ZP and the Village Panchayats. The members of the Panchayat Samiti elect a chairman and a deputy chairman from among the elected members. The Chairman of the Panchayat Samiti is given the power to call for any information or report from any officer or servant working under the Panchayat Samithi. He is also given powers to inspect any movable property in the block or any work or development schemes in progress in the block undertaken by the ZP or the Panchayat Samiti. He presides over the meetings of the Samiti and controls the discussions in the meeting. In fact he is the person on whose imagination and dynamism depends the development of the Block. The post provides him with an opportunity to establish his leadership in his area.

The Block Development Officer, who is an officer of the State Government sent on deputation to the Panchayat Samiti, is the Executive Officer of the Samiti. He also acts as the Secretary to the Committee. All important papers and documents connected with the proceedings of the Samiti meeting are kept in his custody. He draws and disburses money out of the grants. The Samitis have been given functions in the spheres of sanitation, rural health and communications, education and culture, social education, agricultural and animal husbandry, small industries, cooperation, community development, etc. They have been entrusted with responsibilities for primary education, of running dispensaries, maintaining certain roads and of carrying out the Community Development Programmes. They have also been entrusted with certain land revenue powers and functions and execution of relief work and other measures during natural calamities like scarcity, floods, etc.

The lowest tier in the Panchayati Raj structure is at the village level, called Gram Panchayat. Each Gram Panchayat has a minimum of 7 and a maximum of 15 members, all of whom are directly elected. Generally 150-200 voters elect one representative. Each Gram Panchayat is by law required to have at least two women members and seats are reserved for the SCs and STs on the basis of their population. The members of the Gram Panchayat elect a chairman (who is called Sarpanch) from among themselves. The list of functions entrusted to the Gram Panchayat covers a wide range of activities relating to agriculture, animal husbandry, education, sanitation, public works, social welfare, etc. The function of land revenue collection, along with minor coercive powers, is also entrusted to the Gram Panchayats. The Sarpanch is made directly responsible for the fulfilment of the duties imposed upon the Panchayat. In his capacity as Sarpanch, he presides over the meetings of the Gram Panchayat. He keeps the records and registers in his custody and exercises supervision and control over the action taken by the officers and servants of the Panchayat. He is authorised to operate the village fund and issue receipts under his signature for monies received. He is assisted in his work by a Gram Sewak (village level worker) who acts as the secretary to the Panchayat office in the village. The District Collector has been given powers to suspend a Sarpanch against whom criminal proceedings are instituted.

Even though the Naik Committee had recommended that the members of the State Legislature and Parliament should be kept outside the Panchayati Raj bodies, they have been made associate members of the ZP in both the States of Maharashtra and Gujarat. The District Collector (and also the Divisional Commissioner in the case of Maharashtra) has been given supervisory powers over the Panchayati Raj bodies. The planning work in both the States has been entrusted to a body outside the ZP under the chairmanship of a State Government minister. Similarly, most of the Community Development Programmes in both these States are implemented by their respective District Rural Development Societies which are kept outside the PRIs, even though the chief executive officer of the concerned ZP functions as the Chairman of this Society. The financial base of the PRIs in both the States is extremely weak as of now and they have to depend largely on the State Governments for budgetary support.

The West Bengal Model

The West Bengal Panchayat Act, 1973 also provided for a three-tier system consisting of Gram Panchayat (for a small group of villages), Panchayat Samiti (at the Block level) and ZP (at the District level).

The Gram Panchayat had between 5 and 25 members directly elected by the people.Though no constituencies were reserved for the SCs and STs or women, the State Government, on the recommendation of the Gram Panchayat, had powers to nominate to make up the number of the SCs and STs and women members in the Panchayat to two each at least.The Chairman of the Gram Panchayat was elected by the Gram Panchayat members from among themselves.

The Panchayat Samiti, under this Act, consisted of all the chairmen of the Gram Panchayats within the Block, such persons as may be elected from each Gram Panchayat within the Block based on population and the members of the State Legislature falling within the area of the Block. As in the case of the Gram Panchayat the government had the power to nominate two members each from the SCs and STs and two women members, if their number in the Samiti does not come up to two each. The President of the Samithi was elected by the members of the Samiti from amongst themselves.

The ZP consisted of the Presidents of the Panchayat Samitis within the district and two members to be directly elected from each Block. There was a provision for nomination of up to two members from the SCs and STs and two women, as in the case of Panchayats and Panchayat Samitis. The members of the State Legislature and of Parliament within the district were also members of the ZP. The President of the ZP was elected by the members from amongst themselves.

The Left Front Government in West Bengal, elected in 1977, had agreed with the Ashok Mehta Committee's recommendation of officially recognising the participation of political parties at all the levels of the Panchayati Raj and decided to significantly alter the existing Act accepting most of the other recommendations as well. It, however, decided to continue the three-tier structure as against the two-tier system proposed by the committee. The Panchayat elections under the amended Act were conducted for the first time in June 1978, on party basis.

A number of changes were brought about at the organisational level, most notably :– (a) the merger of the Community Development Department with the Department of Panchayats; (b) making the District Magistrate (who is the equivalent of the District Collector in other States) the Chief Executive Officer of the ZP and providing another senior officer of the State Civil Service to work as additional executive officer; (c) statutorily associating all the District and Block-level officers of the different Development Departments with the corresponding Standing Committees of the ZP and Panchyat Samitis respectively; (d) making the block development officer as the executive officer of the Panchayat Samithi to work under the Chairman of the Panchayat Samithi; and (e) the creation of a new accounts and audit organisation in the Department of Panchayats and Community Development to assist the new Panchayati Raj leadership in budgeting, accounting and audit work.The political will to increase the prestige of the PRIs was reflected through various schemes of programme devolution that followed. Most of the development programmes with necessary financial resources were assigned to the PRIs; and as early as 1978-79, the Gram Panchayats were on an average handling Rs. 150,000 each (approximately $15,000 then) and the ZPs Rs. 45 million each (approximately $4.5 million then).

The financial position of the PRIs also improved under this dispensation. To help the Panchayats build up their own funds, the State Government decided to give to the Gram Panchayats a matching grant equivalent to the total cess collected by them every year. In addition, the Government gave away a certain percentage of land revenue collected by the district administration to the Panchayat Samitis. It also agreed to empower the Samitis to control *haats* (local markets), bazars and ferry services, and levy rates upon them; to credit the entire collections of road cess, public works cess, etc., direct to the funds of the ZP concerned without any deduction of collection costs; and to merge the Darjeeling Improvement Fund and such other area development funds with the funds of the ZP concerned. Through an amendment to the Act of 1973 the Panchayat Samitis and ZPs were empowered to borrow money from the State Government, or with the previous sanction of the State Government, from banks or other financial institutions on the basis of specific schemes.[21]

The MLAs and MPs have been made full members of the ZP in West Bengal though they do not become Chairman or Vice-Chairman of either the ZP or any of its Standing Committees. No supervisory powers have been given to the State bureaucracy over any of the PRIs even though the State Government has retained the powers to suspend any resolution of any of the PRIs and also to supersede them if necessary. The law, however, provides for elections to such of those institutions within six months of their supersession. Though most of the development programmes are implemented by the District Rural Development Society in West Bengal as well, the Chairman of a ZP has been made the Chairman of that District Rural Development Society through an administrative order of the State Government. The planning work in West Bengal is, however, entrusted to an outside body which functions under the chairmanship of a State Minister, as in the case of Maharashtra and Gujarat.

Present Scenario

Though many States reacted sharply to the recommendations of the Ashok Mehta Committee, and some critics called the entire exercise of the committee an exercise in futility, it should be said that it created an all-round awareness for reforms in the Panchayati Raj. While some States brought in new Panchayat laws or amended the existing ones, many others at least went for Panchayati Raj polls, which were long overdue. Even the traditional village councils in the north eastern State of Nagaland (corresponding to the statutory Village Panchayats elsewhere), were given powers to deal with development matters in 1978, as a result of which a Village Development Board was created in each village during 1980 – to formulate schemes and programmes for the development and progress of the village or individuals in the village.[22] The board consisted of members representing all clans appointed by the village council, including at least one woman. From amongst them one literate member was chosen as the secretary – the key functionary. The Deputy Commissioner (who acts essentially as a moderator and has the power to exercise a veto over drawal of money from the Village Development Board's bank accounts) was made the chairman of the board.[23]

Alongside the attempts in Karnataka and Andhra Pradesh to create their new PRIs, the G.V.K. Rao Commitee appointed by the National Planning Commission to review the existing administrative arrangements for rural development, strongly recommended for the revival of PRIs all over the country highlighting the inevitable need to transfer power of the State to democratic bodies at the local level.[24] The Government of India then set up a committee in June, 1986, headed by the Constitutional expert Dr. L.M. Singhvi to prepare a concept paper on the revitalisation of the PRIs. The purpose of the paper was to reflect on the process of democratic decentralisation, review the growth and present status and functions of the PRIs and consider the measures required to revitalise these institutions to make them truly effective instruments of self-employment in the constructive task of rural development and nation-building.[25] Among other things, the committee recommended that local self-government should be constitutionally recognised, protected and preserved by the inclusion of a new chapter in the Constitution. It also recommended a constitutional provision to ensure regular, free and fair election for the PRIs and suggested that the task be entrusted to the Election Commission of India.[26]

Accepting these recommendations of the committee, the Rajiv Gandhi Government in 1989 and the V.P.Singh Government in 1990 brought in constitutional amendments to ensure the establishment of local self-governments throughout the country as an acknowledged third tier of the government. Though both these amendments fell through for different reasons, most of the political parties in India had by then agreed in principle to the establishment of viable PRIs all over India despite their differences over details and procedures.

The present government headed by Shri P.V. Narasimha Rao, therefore, introduced a comprehensive amendment bill on September 16, 1991, which was subsequently referred to a Joint Select Committee of Parliament for a detailed examination. The Joint Committee presented their report to Parliament in July 1992. Wide-ranging consultations were held with the representatives of different political parties by the Government on the bill as reported by the Joint Committee and necessary amendments were brought in through a process of consensus. The Bill was finally passed with near unanimity in both Houses of Parliament in December 1992. Following the ratification of the Bill by 17 out of the 20 States which had elected assemblies in position, the President of India gave his assent to the Bill on April 20, 1993, and the Constitution (73rd Amendment) Act, 1992, was brought into effect from April 24, 1993.

Salient Features of the Constitution (73rd Amendment) Act

As enshrined in Article 40 of the Constitution, this Constitution (Amendment) Act envisages the establishment of Panchayats as units of local self-government. Adequate powers and responsibilities would be devolved upon these Panchayats at the appropriate level to enable them to prepare and implement schemes for economic development and social justice. The provisions of this Act, however, do not apply to the States of Nagaland, Meghalaya and Mizoram and also the hill areas of Manipur, which have a traditional system of their own. Its provisions relating to Panchayats at the district level do not apply to the hill areas of the district of Darjeeling in West Bengal for which the Darjeeling Gorkha Council exists.

The Gram Sabha or village council has been envisaged as the foundation of the Panchayati Raj system. It shall perform such functions and exercise such powers as may be entrusted to it by the State legislatures. There shall be three tiers of Panchayats at the village, intermediate and district levels. Only States having a population not exceeding 20 lakhs have the discretion not to constitute the Panchayats at the intermediate level. All seats in a Panchayat at every level are to be filled by direct elections from territorial constituencies demarcated for this purpose, with the ratio between the population of such constituency and the number of seats allotted to it being the same throughout the Panchayat area.

Reservation of seats has been provided at every level for the SCs/STs in proportion to their population in a given Panchayat area and for women to the extent of not less than one-third of the total number of seats. Similarly, offices of the chairpersons in the Panchayats at each level shall be reserved for women, to the extent of not less than one-third of the total number of offices of chairpersons in the Panchayats at each level, and for the SCs and STs in proportion to the population of the SCs/STs in the State as against the total population of the State. In addition, the Legislature of any State can make provision for reservation of seats in any Panchayat or office of chairpersons in the Panchayats at any level in favour of the backward classes of citizens. The term of office of Panchayats at every level shall be for five years and if dissolved earlier, elections must be completed within six months from the date of dissolution. The direction and control of the preparation of electoral rolls and the conduct of all elections in the Panchayats shall be vested in the State Election Commission to be constituted by the State concerned.

Within one year from April 24, 1993, i.e. the coming into effect of the Constitution (73rd Amendment) Act, 1992, and thereafter, at the expiration of every fifth year, a Finance Commission has to be constituted in every State to go into the principles governing the distribution and devolution of financial resources between the State and the Panchayats at every level and the measures to improve the financial position of the Panchayats.

Finally a new schedule called the Eleventh Schedule comprising 29 items has been added to the Constitution which ought to provide an effective role to the PRIs in the planning and implementation of works of local significance ranging from drinking water, agriculture, land and water conservation, to communications, poverty alleviation programmes, family welfare, education, libraries and cultural activities, maintenance of community assets, etc. The constitution of District Planning Committees and strengthening of the administrative machinery at the level of all Panchayats will hopefully ensure timely preparation of development plans on matters of common interest including spatial planning, implementation of development projects relevant to their physical and natural resources and integrated development of infrastructure and environmental conservation.

Conclusion

The Constitution (73rd Amendment) Act, 1992, has broken a distinctly new ground. The PRIs that will now be established in India deserve to succeed at least as the principal vehicles for rural development. The essential prerequisites for their success are the political will and the administrative back-up. The political will at the Central level has been exhibited by the unanimous adoption of the Constitution (Amendment) Bill. It is expected that the State level will also follow this up by amending their respective (Panchayat) Acts within the prescribed time-frame, preferably through a process of consensus. A great deal of responsibility will still rest on the political leaders at the national and State levels to provide proper guidance to the newly elected representatives in the PRIs.

Problems are bound to surface when there is a major change in the political and administrative system, but these problems are by no means insoluble. With proper understanding and appreciation by both the polity and the bureaucracy, the PRIs can develop as vigorous institutions of local self-government. The economic development through various programmes that are to be taken up during the Eighth Five Year Plan, which has a massive provision for rural development, has to be channelised by provision of adequate funds to the PRIs. With the active involvement of the grassroot organisations, both in planning and in implementation, the face of rural India will favourably change, bringing about the long-cherished goal of growth with social justice. The quality of implementation will also improve as the PRIs are ideally suited for effective implementation of the programmes entrusted to them.

All these will pose a lot of challenges and also provide opportunities. And the success would lie in converting the challenges into opportunities. The next few years are, therefore, crucial for the development of the PRIs and also the Indian democracy, through them.

NOTES AND REFERENCES

1. Jawaharlal Nehru, *The Discovery of India*, Signet Press, Calcutta, 1964, p. 288.
2. *Imperial Gazetteer of India* (1909), Vol. 4, p. 278.
3. *Report of the royal commission on decentralisation,* 1907.
4. Gandhiji, "My idea of village swaraj", *Harijan*, 26-7-1942.
5. *Constituent Assembly Debates*, 4-11-1948.
6. Gandhiji, *Harijan*, 21-12-1947.
7. *Constituent Assembly Debates,* 5-11-1948, Sri H.V. Kamath.
8. *Ibid.*, 9-11-1948, Prof. N.G. Ranga.
9. *The First Five Year Plan,* Planning Commission, Government of India, 1953, p. 133.
10. *The Second Five Year Plan,* Planning Commission, Government of India, 1956, p. 148.
11. *A study of panchayat*, Government of India, May, 1958.
12. *Report of the team for the study of community projects and national extension services,* 1959.
13. *Report of the G.V.K. Rao committee on administrtive arrangements for rural development,* 1985.
14. L.P. Shukla, *A history of village panchayats in India,* Institute of Economic Research, Dharwar, 1964.
15. *Ashok Mehta Committee Report,* 1978.
16. W.A. Robson, *Local government in crisis,* George Allen and Unwin, London, 1966. p. 50.
17. *Report on India's food crisis and measures to meet it,* 1959.
18. Dr. B.S. Bhargava, *Panchayati Raj movement in India,* Institute of Social and Economic Change, Bangalore. 1985.
19. *Ashok Mehta Committee Report, op. cit.*
20. *Naik committee report,* Government of Maharashtra, 1961.
21. A.K. Mukhopadhyay, *The Panchayat Administration in West Bengal.* The World Press Private Limited, Culcutta, 1980.
22. Village Development Boards Rules 1980, Government of Nagaland, Rule 3.
23. Ibid., Rules 4, 6, 7 and 20.
24. *G.V.K. Rao Committee Report, op. cit.*
25. L.M. Singhvi *Committee Report,* 1986. para 1.3
26. *Ibid.*, paras 7.1 and 8.2.

5

THE KARNATAKA MODEL

History

At the time of reorganisation of the Indian States in 1956 the south-western State of Karnataka (then called Mysore) in peninsular India inherited different local self-government laws from the States from which the reorganised State was carved. Following the Balwantrai Mehta Committee report and the central directive, the first attempt at an uniform legislation was made through the Karnataka Village Panchayats and Local Boards Act, 1959. The Panchayati Raj system then provided a three-tier structure, spatially speaking – Village Panchayat/Town Panchayat at village/group of villages level; Taluk Development Board at the block level; and District Development Council at district level. The Village/Town Panchayats were directly elected tiers with no "organic linkage" and the District Development Council was mainly a bureaucratic tier having an organic linkage with the Taluk Development Board in the sense that the presidents of these boards in the district were also members of the District Development Council (in addition to the members of Legislature and Parliament). An indirectly elected chairman was provided for the Village/Town Panchayat and the Taluk Development Board but the Deputy Commissioner (or the District Collector) was made the ex-officio president of the District Development Council.

The functions of the Village/Town Panchayats as well as the Taluk Development Boards were incorporated in the Act whereas the District Development Council was simply a coordinating and supervising body which approved the budgets of the Taluk Development Boards but had no other executive functions. No Plan/non-Plan schemes or staff were transferred to these elected bodies, though these bodies were utilized by the State administration to implement local plan schemes and the Block Development Officer was the chief executive officer of the Taluk Development Board. In the planning and development process, they were almost entirely implementing bodies and not plan formulating bodies.

In 1962, with a view to conferring real powers and resources on the PRIs to fall in line with the concept of democratic decentralisation which the Balwantrai Mehta Committee recommended for adoption, the State Government constituted a committee under the chairmanship of Shri Kondajji Basappa to recommend a structure suited to the needs of the State, which submitted its report in 1963. Accepting the recommendations of the committee the State Government introduced a Bill in 1964 to establish a three-tier structure of rural self-government in the then Mysore State. The select committee headed by the then Rural Development Minister, Shri Ramakrishna Hegde, enthusiastically recommended enhanced powers to the PRIs but nothing came out of it as neither the ruling party nor the Government was prepared for launching such an experiment then. Karnataka had only three Panchayati Raj elections in the course of 25 years, first in 1960, second in 1968 and third in 1978. Originally their term was for four years but later on was amended to five years. In 1983, on the expiry of their term, administrators were appointed by the Government to discharge the functions of these PRIs.

When the Janata Party was voted to power in the State of Karnataka in 1983, the Government headed by Shri Ramakrishna Hegde had a political reason to go in for a radical Panchayati Raj system in Karnataka. Firstly, it was Shri Ramakrishna Hegde himself who had piloted and vehemently defended the 1964 Bill that had fallen through. In his new capacity as the Chief Minister, he had to show his will once again. Secondly, it was the Janata Government at the Centre which had appointed the Ashok Mehta Committee whose recommendations could not be implemented because of the untimely fall of the Government. What the party could not get through at the Central level had to be attempted at least at the State level where it had gained power. It can also be a way of distinguishing a Janata Government from the State Governments run by the Congress, besides building up local cadres for the party. Thirdly, the Janata Party had made a clear-cut promise in their election manifesto to the people of Karnataka that they would strive to usher in a radical Panchayati Raj system in the State if voted to power and they found it difficult to go back on the same.

Besides the political necessity, the Government of Karnataka had two other reasons to go in for the Panchayati Raj system. One was economic and the other administrative. Over three decades of independence had no doubt brought the district headquarters town and the taluk centres to some level of economic development, but this had not percolated down below. There was a need to identify potential growth centres which could be consciously developed. The headquarters of the Mandal Panchayat (suggested by the Ashok Mehta Committee) would be an ideal growth centre for provision of necessary developmental infrastructure as well as for the efficient management of the growing rural-urban linkages.

At the time of independence every district in the country had a District Collector or a Deputy Commissioner or a District Magistrate who was the chief representative of the State Government at the district level. He was essentially in charge of collection of revenue and maintenance of law and order. When the focus of the independent India shifted from maintenance of public order to development, instead of creating a separate set of bureaucrats to deal with the problems of development, the District Collector was given the additional responsibility of executing and supervising development functions as well. Despite all cosmetic changes such as the creation of special agencies to execute specific development programmes like the Small Farmers' Development Agency (SFDA), the Drought Prone Area Programme (DPAP), etc., the Collector always continued to be the central figure in the development of the district as the chairman of most of these agencies. The debate as to whether such an officer at the district level, over-burdened as he is with all types of activities ranging from law and order to rural development, can really deliver the goods has been continuing.

The Government of Karnataka, however, felt that the time had come to decisively break away from this tradition and bifurcate the management of regulatory and development functions performed by the District Collector. Karnataka was the only State in India where the District Collector had been entirely kept out of the Panchayati Raj system and another officer, not below the rank of the District Collector (designated as the Chief Secretary of the Zilla Parishad), was entrusted with the discharge of all development functions under the ZP, without having to report to the collector at any point of time. In effect, the role of the District Collector in Karnataka had been reduced to that of the pre-independence collector of a district and the development responsibilities were entirely taken over by the PRIs.

Structure and Functions

The Karnataka Zilla Parishads, Taluk Panchayat Samitis, Mandal Panchayats and Nyaya Panchayats Act, 1983 (hereafter, the Karnataka Act) which received Presidential assent on July 10, 1985, clearly mentioned in the preamble that the purpose of establishing these local bodies was essentially to assign to them local government and judicial functions and to entrust the execution of certain works and development schemes of the State Five Year Plans. The Karnataka Act provided for the decentralisation of powers and functions "for the purpose of promoting the development of democratic institutions and securing a greater measure of participation by the people".[1] Despite the fact that, following the Constitution (73rd Amendment) Act 1992, the Karnataka Act was repealed and replaced by a new Act on May 10, 1993, the system this Act had established deserves a closer look from the point of view of its adaptability elsewhere. We shall, therefore, examine the details of the Karnataka model which came into being during 1987 and functioned for a full term of five years thereafter.

Though the Karnataka Act was largely based on the recommendations of the Ashok Mehta Committee in as much as it provided for only two elected tiers of decentralisation, there were as many as five different layers in the system that finally became fully operational on April 1, 1987. The Gram Sabha (village council) was the basic unit of the system and comprised all eligible voters, that is, all persons above the age of 18 years, of that village. The Gram Sabha, which by law had to meet at least twice a year, was expected to discuss and review all development problems/programmes of the village, select beneficiaries for all beneficiary oriented programmes transferred to the Panchayati Raj system, plan for local improvement, including minimum needs, welfare and production oriented programmes including the cropping pattern for the season for the village, etc. and constitute the land army consisting of all able-bodied persons to whom employement would have to be provided under the various development schemes taken up in the locality. It was presided over by the Chairman of the Mandal Panchayat, to which the village belonged. Attendance of senior officers for every Gram Sabha meeting, keeping of records of the discussion and monitoring action thereon had been insisted upon.[2]

The Mandal Panchayat was the first elected tier of the system. It was entrusted with all civic functions and powers and responsibility for development and welfare programmes with an intra-Mandal orientation. It covered a group of villages with a population, as per the 1981 census, between 8,000 and 12,000 suitably reduced for the hill areas[3] (on an average a Mandal covered approximately 10 to 11 villages and the distance between the Mandal headquarters and any of its villages did not usually exceed 10 kilometres). One representative was elected on party basis for a term of five years by every 400 population (or approximately 80 households); 25 per cent of the membership had been earmarked for women (of whom at least one should belong to the SC/ST) and 18 per cent or more for SC/STs depending upon their actual population within the Mandal. The Chairman and the Vice-chairman of the Mandal were elected by its members. Karnataka under this system had 2,536 Mandals with 55,188 elected members.[4]

A Mandal Panchayat performed three different types of functions : obligatory, discretionary and transferred. It was the duty of the Panchayat to make reasonable provisions within the village regarding sanitation and health, which included construction and maintenance of wells and tanks, supply of water, sanitation, provision of public latrines, etc.; and some regulatory functions, such as regulation of buildings and shops, of the curing, tanning and dyeing of skins and hides. Obligatory functions also included construction, repair and maintenance of roads, drains, bunds, regulation of grazing lands of the villages and so on. It was the duty of the Mandal Panchayat to formulate and prepare agricultural production plans for its area including the establishment of nurseries and storage of improved seeds, pesticides, etc., propagation of improved methods of cultivation and related activity. An important duty cast on the Panchayat was the promotion of educational, economic, social, cultural and other interests of the Scheduled Castes, Tribes and Backward Classes.

Discretionary functions were couched in general, enabling terms so that any other work or measure which was likely to promote the health, safety, education or general well-being of the people could be taken up. Transferred functions were those assigned by the government, for instance, management of forests, wasteland cultivation, etc. The Mandal Panchayat functioned through three standing committees, namely, a production committee concerned with agriculture, animal husbandry and rural industry; a social justice committee to look after the interests of the scheduled castes and tribes, backward classes and women; and an amenities committee to perform functions in respect of education, public health and public works.

At the next higher level was the Taluk Panchayat Samiti located at the existing Block headquarters, which was a purely nominated body comprising ex-officio all the chairmen of the Mandals in the Block; all members of the State Legislature representing any part of the Block (excluding urban areas), members of the ZP representing any part of the Block, president of the Taluk Agricultural Producers Cooperative Marketing Society and president of the primary agricultural and rural development bank, besides five members belonging to the scheduled castes, scheduled tribes, backward classes and women by co-option with the approval of the ZPs. The MLA representing the major part of the taluk was the chairman of the Taluk Panchayat Samiti. This body was entrusted with advisory, supervisory, review and inter-Mandal co-ordination functions *vis-a-vis* the Mandals of the taluk.

The creation of a Taluk Panchayat Samiti was never contemplated either in the Ashok Mehta Committee report or in the original scheme of things envisaged under the Karnataka pattern of decentralisation. It sprang more as a political necessity – to ensure the support of the members of the State Legislature in the smooth passage of the Karnataka Act which was piloted by a minority government – than on a matter of principle. The Taluk Panchayat Samiti was, therefore, deliberately designed to be a purely advisory body, with no powers, functions or even a legal identity in as much as it could neither sue nor be sued against.

The Zilla Parishad (ZP) was the second directly elected tier of this model. Its functions, responsibilities and powers were so formulated as to render it unambiguously the head of the district's development and welfare administration.[5] It had jurisdiction over the entire district, excluding the urban areas. ZPs had one elected representative for every 28,000 population (except the hill district of Kodagu which had one seat for every 12,000 population) and reservations had been provided for women and scheduled castes and scheduled tribes as in the case of Mandals.[6] Elections were held on a party basis and the term of office was five years.

Members of Parliament and members of the State Legislature whose constituencies cover the district or a part thereof were members of the ZP but did not have the right to hold any office in the ZP. The chairman/president of the District Central Cooperative Bank will be an associate member. He could take part in the meetings of the ZP, but could not vote. The chairman (Adhyaksha) and the vice-chairman (Upadhyaksha) of the ZP were elected by the members of the ZP. The Adhyaksha of the ZP had the rank of a Minister of State and

Upadhyaksha the rank of a Deputy Minister. The Adhyaksha had been declared the executive head of the ZP.

Under this system, the ZP administered schemes and programmes transferred to it or evolved by it; maintained cadres for manning the ZP and mandal staff; formulated the district plan; framed and approved its budget; and approved the budgets of the mandals. On the constitution of the ZP all the district rural development societies were dissolved and their functions (along with their assets and liabilities) transferred to the respective ZPs. There were nine standing committees, one each for finance and audit, planning and development, public works and amenities, social justice, education, agriculture and animal husbandry, health, industries and a general standing committee to implement and monitor the multi-faced activities of the ZP. The members of these standing committees were elected by the members of the ZP from among themselves, in accordance with the system of proportional representation by means of single transferable vote. No member of the ZP was allowed to serve on more than two standing committees.[7]

At the apex of this Panchayati Raj system was the State Development Council, which was chaired by the Chief Minister of the State and comprised the chairmen of all the ZPs in the State, six Ministers of the State and the Development Commissioner as member-secretary. It was to meet once a quarter and provided a forum for continuous review and direction of the Panchayati Raj movement in the State, in addition to providing a sounding board for policy and procedural formulations as also interaction between the State political executive and the PRIs.

An interesting feature of the Karnataka model described above is the relative freedom given to each tier in the system and the organic linkages it provides for. The State has retained over the ZPs only the power of dissolution for excess or abuse of their powers, persistent default in or incompetence to perform their statutory duties. Reconstitution by election is mandatory within six months of such dissolution. In respect of Mandals, the ZP has the similar power of dissolving the Mandal plus the power to approve the annual budget and the power to suspend any resolution or order of the Mandal or its officers. Here, too, reconstitution by election is mandatory within six months.[8] There is a conscious effort to ensure that the Mandals function autonomously, independent of the ZPs, just as the ZPs are expected to function autonomously, independent of the State Government. However, observance of national and State priorities and observance of statutes is insisted upon. Significantly the State has not stipulated any priorities to which the PRIs are required to conform, save those which flow from the national priorities, like the minimum needs programme, earmarked funds, etc.

The extent of autonomy statutorily ensured to the ZPs and Mandals is unique in the Karnataka system. For instance, (1) no government officer can suspend a resolution of a Mandal or a ZP; (2) there is no provision to declare the Divisional Commissioner or for that matter any other government officer as the controlling officer; (3) subject to budgetary ceilings and national/State priorities set by the Government of India/Planning Commission, plans/budgets formulated by the mandals are not amended by the ZP/State Government. Similarly the district plans of the ZPs incorporating *inter alia* such Mandal plans are not amended by the State Government; (4) there is no apex body above the ZP like the District Planning Board or the District Planning and Development Council; (5) the chairman of the ZP is also made the chairman of the Karnataka Development Programme Committee for the district which meets every month and reviews all planned programmes as also action under all other major areas of development and related activities. (Its membership in fact includes not only the ZP chief secretary and district heads of all development departments under the ZP, but also the Deputy Commissioner, the district heads of other departments of the State Government, district heads of statutory bodies, lead banks, service undertakings, etc.).[9]

To secure speedy and inexpensive justice in civil and criminal matters of a relatively minor nature, Nyaya Panchayats have been envisaged under this Act. It comprises five members of whom not less than three will belong to the reserved categories which are generally accepted as weaker sections of society, namely, scheduled castes and scheduled tribes, backward classes and women.[10] Having regard to the delicate and sensitive nature of this authority, safeguards have been introduced by the statute, such as the subject matter of the suit or the case be of a very minor nature; exclusion of imprisonment from its competence; exclusion of lawyers from the proceedings, the majority of the Nyaya Panchayat's membership comprising acknowledgedly weaker sections of the population, etc. According to a government publication, "the effectiveness of a social sanction, the widespread experience that truth surfaces locally without elaborate evidentiary procedures; the salutary effect of shortening the span between the crime and punishment, injury and redress; need to be utilised in any system of decentralised democratic administration. That is the major rationale leading to these provisions".[11] However, a conscious decision was taken by the then Government of Karnataka to bring the Nyaya Panchayats into effect five years after the commencement of the Panchayati Raj system, by which time the working and credibility of the new PRIs would have stabilised (though this did not happen, following a change of government at the State level. The new Karnataka Panchayati Raj Act, 1993 does not even make a mention of Nyaya Panchayats).

Resources – Financial and Human

Let us now look at the resources that were provided for, in this model. On the financial side, the Mandal Panchayat fund consisted of allotments by the Government or the ZP; proceeds from tax on buildings, entertainment, markets; levy of water rates, etc. In comparison with the long list of functions the resources are meagre. Evidently a substantial part of the Mandal Panchayat fund has to come from the Central/State Governments. Under the statute the State Government was required to make a grant at the rate of Rs. 10 per person residing in the mandal calculated on the basis of the last preceding census of which figures are available.[12] However, 25 per cent of this amount should have to be paid by the government to the ZP. Thus, for a Mandal with a population of 10,000 the general or untied grant would be Rs 75,000 ($ 3,700 then). This and the average collection of taxes of around Rs. 20,000 ($ 1000 then) per annum constituted the main source of finance for the Mandal Panchayats.

The ZP fund consisted of the amounts transferred to the ZP by appropriation from out of the Consolidated Fund of the State; all grants, assignments, loans and contributions made by the State Government; all levies and penalties paid to or levied by or on behalf of the ZP; all rents from land and other properties of the ZP, etc.[13] ZPs did not have powers to levy taxes or cesses, but had powers to raise their own resources by borrowings, investments and remunerative assets. They retained all accruals from income-generating schemes which were transferred to them by the State Government.

The State Government had effected from its budget a massive transfer of resources to the district sector. It constituted the bulk of the ZP/Mandal resources. The sectoral allocations for the district sector were distinctly provided in the State budget. The district-wise allocation thereof was provided in a link document which formed an integral part of the budget documents. The ZP had freedom, within the national discipline of earmarking of funds for specific sectors, to make inter-sectoral reallocations of the funds so transferred to it. In 1988-89 the total district sector provision budgetted for transfer to the PRIs was Rs. 873 crores ($ 437 million then) including Rs. 240 crores ($ 120 million) from the plan budget (which accounts for roughly 30 per cent of the total State Plan outlay), thus providing on an average Rs. 40-45 crores (about $ 2 million per annum) per ZP.[14]

There was a statutory provision in the Karnataka Act for setting up a finance commission every five years to determine the principles on which the resources were to be shared between the State Government and the PRIs and the basis on which allocations would be made among the ZPs/Mandals.[15] The accounts of the ZPs and Mandal Panchayats were audited at least once in every year, by the State accountant general and the controller of State accounts respectively and the audit reports were to be sent not only to the respective ZP/Mandal Panchayats, but also to the next higher institution, namely, the State Government/the ZP concerned.[16]

The official machinery of the ZP was headed by its chief secretary. The post was encadred to the Indian Administrative Service and had been given the status and powers of a major head of the department.[17] The Chief Secretary of the ZP was invariably senior in rank to the Deputy Commissioner of the district who continued to be responsible for regulatory functions which were vested with the State Government. Each ZP had a strong accounting and internal audit set up under a chief Accounts Officer who was drawn from the State accounts department.[18] It also had a planning cell of experts headed by a Chief Planning Officer. The district level officers, with their supporting staff, of all developmental departments had been brought under the ZP.[19]

More than 50 per cent of the 450,000 State Government employees were on deputation in the ZPs. While the senior staff (Group A and Group B) continued to be on deputation from the concerned government departments, steps to permanently absorb or directly recruit the junior cadres (Group C and Group D) by the ZPs, including senior staff of the Mandal Panchayats, who would be from the regular ZP cadres, had been initiated. Each Mandal had a secretary and the village extension worker/agricultural assistant on deputation from the State Government for the time being. Mandals were given the powers to locally appoint other sub-ordinate category staff with the prior approval of the ZP to meet strictly local needs.[20]

The Andhra Model

Around the same time Andhra Pradesh, an adjoining State in southern India, enacted its new Panchayat Act which came into force on January 15, 1987,[21] opting for a three-tier system – the Gram Panchayat at the village level, the Mandala Praja Parishad (MPP) at the intermediate level called Mandal, having a population of about 35,000 to 50,000 (displacing the erstwhile Panchayat Samitis at the Block level) and the Zilla Praja Parishad (ZPP) at the district level. While the chairman and the vice-chairman of each of these bodies were directly elected by the people of the respective units,[22] only the Gram Panchayats had directly elected members as well. Others had only nominated members consisting usually of the chairmen of the lower-level bodies and also the concerned members of the State Legislature and the Parliament. Like Maharashtra, Gujarat and West Bengal States there was a separate district rural development society in Andhra Pradesh also, handling the rural development schemes in the district, besides the District Planning and Development Review Board presided over by a State Government Minister. The primacy of the District Collector had also been protected by making him an ex-officio member of the ZPP (with certain emergency powers over the ZPP) and also the chairman of the district rural development society. The State Government had retained the powers to cancel or suspend any resolution of the MPP/ZPP, under certain circumstances, in addition to the power to supersede or dissolve any of these bodies and appoint a special officer to exercise the powers and perform the functions of any of these bodies and their office bearers.[23]

Evaluation

The performance of the PRIs in Karnataka during their first term in office has evoked a mixed response. While some evaluation reports mention significant achievements during this short period, such as "attendance of school teachers, medical officers, para-medical staff in rural institutions improved remarkably; revenues from assets transferred to these bodies, such as auction of fishing rights in tanks have jumped up; financial improprieties by mandal office-bearers have been exposed in Gram Sabhas and culprits have made good the losses caused or gains wrongfully obtained",[24] some others feel that the process of election on a party basis has deepened the polarisations already existing within the village community endangering peace in some cases. There is also a feeling that the social and political consequences of decentralisation will be to strengthen vested interests in rural areas, promote exploitation of the weaker sections and further enhance corruption at the local level.

I had the good fortune of watching this system function, during the first two years of its operation, at close quarters. Most of us in the bureaucracy had our doubts, at least in the initial months, as to whether such institutions can be creative. Shri Abdul Nazir Sab, the Minister who was responsible for this experiment in Karnataka, insisted on my visiting each one of the 19 ZPs in the State (besides a few Mandal Panchayats), with a team of experts in finance, planning and rural development management, to understand the field problems first-hand from the elected and appointed local government officials and to recommend corrective measures wherever necessary. He also accompanied us to a few ZPs and participated in all the discussions at the divisional level – to review, at a time, the activities of the four or five ZPs within that division. This gave us a fairly reliable insight into the functioning of these institutions, their strength and also shortcomings.

On the positive side, it must be mentioned at the outset that public awareness of the developmental programmes these institutions have created is phenomenal. A geographical area, consisting of about 2,000 households, had 25 elected members, who constituted the Mandal Panchayat for that area. Since the selection of beneficiaries in respect of self-employment schemes and the location of infrastructural facilities were decided finally by the Mandal Panchayat after a thorough discussion, all its members, per force, are to be well conversant with the different developmental activities of the State that are going on within their Mandal. The interest shown by them in the execution of schemes by the ZP functionaries was equally encouraging. Virtually in all ZPs, the operation of schools and health facilities had vastly improved. Performance in the fields of inland fisheries, horticulture, forests and distribution of house sites to the needy had also been good.

The management of the assets transferred to the PRIs was much better than what it used to be under the State departments.There were several instances of a quantum jump in the revenues through increased output of fish in small tanks, horticulture and forest produce etc., Generally development works were being executed more speedily and there was better control over the field staff.

Another noticeable feature is the all-round enthusiasm shown by the people in the activities of the local government. Under the earlier system, people had to wait on the usually busy Deputy Commissioner to explain their development needs and seek redressal. Many of them were left dissatisfied at the end of the interview, as neither they could be given adequate time by the Deputy Commissioner to explain their problems nor could they express themselves adequately before him within the time allotted to them. They also had no way to find out the action taken on their requests, except by going to the office of the Deputy Commissioner once again and seeking another interview – which was both costly and time-consuming. Under the Panchayat system, the chairman of the Mandal Panchayat and the members of the ZP were generally available to the people and the constraint of time did not really exist. The monthly meetings of the mandal as well as the Gram Sabha provided an adequate forum for discussion on local needs and the necessary follow-up, besides ensuring better accountability of the elected members of the local bodies as well as their bureaucrats.

However in some areas, little or no interest in attending Gram Sabhas or accepting Mandal Panchayat as an effective local authority was noticeable. Since the resources available to the Mandal Panchayat were extremely poor when compared to the functions entrusted to it, the tendency appeared to be to treat only the ZP as an effective local government that can deliver the goods. In many Mandals, the Gram Sabhas had not been convened regularly, as the Mandal Panchayats feared that they could not meet the growing demands of the people. A better course would have been to enforce through legislative means the Gram Sabha meetings at least twice a year as prescribed, so that the people could be taken into confidence, on the resources and capabilities of the Mandal Panchayat.

The absence of proper operational linkages between the Mandal Panchayat and the ZP was also felt, especially by the former as the Taluk Panchayat Samiti was found totally inadequate for the purpose. Restructuring of the functions and responsibilities of the Taluk Panchayat Samiti and integrating it as a regular tier in the system as has now been done through the Karnataka Panchayati Raj Act, 1993, will perhaps improve the organisational capability of the entire system. There is also a case for reducing the number of committees at the ZP level and also the frequency of their meeting, as otherwise substantial time of the ZP functionaries would be consumed by these meetings, leaving very little time for field work.

Though the relationship between the officials and the electd representatives has vastly improved over the years, some of the officials and the legislators still have some mental reservations about the scheme of decentralisation. An unequivocal commitment by the State Government, to the progressive devolution of powers to the PRIs is absolutely necessary, at least until these nascent institutions stabilise.

Reconciling the process of decentralisation with comprehensive national planning has been a problem in some districts especially since the financial independence of the PRIs has by no means been assured. Though the State Government had been regularly effecting a substantial transfer of funds to the district sector, through its own budget, one cannot ignore the fact that what can be given by one government can as well be taken away by another.

Finally, there is a widespread feeling that the State level political leaders and the bureaucracy would not tolerate any exercise of local powers by the elected members of these PRIs. Anyway, the declared objectives in setting up these local governments are decentralisation of powers and functions to promote democratic institutions and to secure greater participation by the people in local and governmental affairs. Clearly, a change of this nature takes a considerably longer period to achieve its objectives.

Conclusion

It can thus be seen that among the various Indian models the Karnataka model carried the process of democratic decentralisation the farthest and had, therefore, evoked considerable interest. While the ZPs had the complete responsibility for the overall planning and development of the district, the Mandal Panchayat had a definite role in programme implementation, specially in the selection of beneficiaries in the beneficiary-oriented programmes and location decisions in respect of new physical facilities. Local level planning was also more effective.

The new generation of elected PRIs in Karnataka had completed their term of five years in January, 1992, and went out of office thereafter. Meanwhile, the Congress Government that was voted to power in the State during November, 1989, did bring in a series of amendments to the Karnataka Act, with a view to bringing it closer to the Maharashtra-Gujarat model. Pending consideration of these amendments by the State Legislature and the national pattern that may emerge after the passing of the Constitution Amendment by Parliament, formally providing a constitutional status to the PRIs, senior civil servants were appointed by the State Government during January, 1992, as administrators to discharge the powers and responsibilities of the PRIs throughout the State of Karnataka. Though the State Government has mentioned that this would be a short-term arrangement, it has so far continued beyond twenty months. Now that the new Karnataka Panchayat Raj Act, 1993, which provides for all the mandatory provisions of the Constitution (73rd amendment) Act, 1992, has come into effect, the elections to the new PRIs are likely to be held by early 1994 and elected bodies will hopefully be in position at the village, taluk and district levels within the next few months. The Panchayati Raj system in Karnataka is thus in transition. Whether the new PRIs will prove to be better than their predecessors remains to be seen.

NOTES AND REFERENCES

1. *The Karnataka Zilla Parishads, Taluk Panchayat Samithis, Mandal Panchayats and Nyaya Panchayats Act 1983*, p 1.
2. "Karnataka shows the way", *District governments and decentralised planning*, Government of Karnataka publication, 1988, p. 7.
3. The Karnataka Act, *op. cit.* Section 4 (1).
4. "Karnataka shows the way", *op. cit.*, p. 7.
5. *Ibid.*, p. 7.
6. The Karnataka Act, *op. cit.*, Sections 140, 142 and 143.
7. *Ibid.*, Section 177.
8. *Ibid.*, Section 271.
9. Unfortunately, most of these provisions have been watered down in the Karnataka Panchayat Raj Act, 1993 which has given substantial powers of inspection and supervision to the State Government officers. A district planning committee has also been constituted as envisaged under the Constitution (74th Amendment) Act, 1992 relating to Municipalities, to consolidate the plans prepared by the PRIs and the municipal bodies in the district.
10. The Karnataka Act, *op. cit.*, Section 212.
11. "Karnataka shows the way", *op. cit.*, p. 15.
12. The Karnataka Act, *op. cit.*, Section 114 (3).
13. *Ibid.*, Section 191.
14. "Karnataka shows the way", *op. cit.* p. 9.
15. The Karnataka Act, *op. cit.*, Section 210.
16. *Ibid.*, Section 205.
17. "Karnataka shows the way", *op. cit.*, p. 8.
18. The Karnataka Act, *op. cit.*, Section 174.
19. *Ibid.*, Section 184.
20. *Ibid.*, Section 123.
21. The Andhra Pradesh Mandala Praja Parishads, Zilla Praja Parishads and Zilla Abhivrudhi Sameeksha Mandals Act, 1986.
22. *Ibid.*, Section 44.
23. *Ibid.*, Section 75.
24. See *Report of the Zilla Parishads and Mandal Panchayats Evaluation Committee*. Government of Karnataka, March 1989.

6

STRUCTURE AND RELATIONSHIPS

The institutional design for decentralisation should take into account not only the developmental thrusts built upon the capabilities at the local levels but also the need to ensure local participation in decision-making. The emerging scenario of the dynamics of development in most countries necessitates that the technical expertise of a high order be made available at levels below the State/Province to sustain the momentum of development which, in many cases, has been already administratively decentralised at the district/county level. The inescapable compulsion, therefore, is that the district/county should be the first point of decentralisation, under popular supervision, below the State level.[1] Though there are administrative "divisions" in some States in India, comprising a few districts and the system of Prefecture (Di), comprising a few counties in China, it is admitted in both the countries that these are only locations for the establishment of Central Government public offices and the real centre of local power always lies with the district/county.

The problem of striking a balance between technological requirements and possibilities for meaningful participation by the people in development management occurs at levels below the district/county. Since it is extremely difficult, in many countries, to combine representativeness and viability in one level of local government, this problem is sought to be solved by having two or more tiers in such a way that the smaller-area one is closer to the people while the larger-area one is better financed and technically more powerful. For the time being, Nigeria has a single-tier system of local governments covering the entire area of a county. The development areas constituted under the county are, at best, administrative offices of the local governments concerned. China has a well-defined township/town government (xiang/zhen) below the county level, for a population of 30,000 to 50,000 on an average, with a Village Committee for each village, which functions purely as a self-managing organ outside the government. While most States in India have opted for a two-tier system, below the district level – a Taluk Panchayat Samiti at the block level for a population of about 100,000 to 150,000 and a Gram Panchayat for a single or a group of villages, with a population of 3,000 to 5,000 – a few States have only a single tier, a Mandal Panchayat covering a group of villages. The population of a mandal varies from an average of 10,000 in Karnataka to around 40,000 in Andhra Pradesh.

The question of adequate area for a unit of administration is quite complicated in any given country, owing to unevenness in terms of economic resources, communication facilities, population density, level of social integration, civic commitment, etc. A uniform set of criteria cannot apply, even within a single country. It would, therefore, seem appropriate to leave the exact pattern of local government below the district/county level to the States/provinces. The Central/Federal Government could at best lay down a general criteria for their guidance.

More recently two criteria have been suggested for determining the size of a local government unit. These are access and service.[2] If service is taken as the prime determinant of size, the most important consideration is the population base needed to carry out effective local government programmes, because the cost of the service is a function of the population requiring that service, although at some point, when the population reaches a certain level, the unit cost of the service would reduce. It means, therefore, a minimum and a maximum population can be established – a minimum to guarantee that the service is not too expensive and consequently inaccessible to the people and a maximum to ensure quality and promptness in service.

Access to government in terms of influencing public policy decisions and enhancing both responsible and responsive administration is a prime requirement for any democratic government. If access is an important prerequisite of size, then, in addition to population, one has to look at the communication network, level of political awareness, and also the area. While the service criteria will take care of the economic viability and administrative efficiency, the access criteria should serve the political and democratic needs of the people. Should the application of these criteria lead to divergent views, then one has to raise the basic query, whether the functions of local government can be or should be performed for profit.

Insisting on viability for local government and not for other levels of government would amount to an obvious discrimination against local government since the local government provides an instrument for democracy or at least provides an extra avenue for democratic participation – even the Village Committee law adopted by China aims at "promoting socialist democracy at the grass-roots level".[3] The "access" criteria should, therefore, precede the "service" criteria in determining the structure of local government institutions in any country. If that be so, keeping in view the area size and population in Nigeria, China and India, a two-tier system below the district/county level might seem appropriate in most parts of these countries to ensure effective participation by the people in local decision-making.

It must, however, be added that the lowest tier should not be so small in size as to make it insignificant or incapable of discharging its legitimate duties as a local government. For instance, the Village Panchayats in most parts of India, covering a population of about 2,500 cannot perform any functions on their own and hence do not command the respect a local government deserves. Even the Mandal Panchayats of Karnataka (which covered a population of about 10,000 on an average) suffered from poor resources, both financial and human, and hence depended heavily on the Zilla Parishad. The Mandal Praja Parishads in Andhra Pradesh, with a population of about 40,000, appear to satisfy both the access and service criteria and have the potential of becoming the growth centres which can discharge the duties of a local government, closer to the people, fairly effectively, at least in Indian conditions.

At this stage it is perhaps necessary to look at whether mere constitution of local government institutions at appropriate levels, holding of regular elections and even providing representation to women and weaker sections (as has been done in India), would by themselves mean, or at least lead to, effective "participation" by the people. In the context of the concept of "power to the people" degenerating into "power to the powerful" in many democracies, the elected representatives not bothering to meet their electorate even once during their term of office and still getting re-elected on the strength of their party label and a substantial portion of the constituency not turning up to exercise their franchise out of sheer disgust on the polling day, how can democratic decentralisation through local government institutions be ensured? Local government institutions are often criticised for helping the dominant caste/group in the society to further consolidate their hold over the non-dominant and minority groups. In a society where control of land leads to control of levers of power (which is largely true in

Nigeria and India) will not the local government institutions be more accessible to the upper strata of the society?

A recent study on the social background of the Zilla Parishad Presidents in Karnataka came to the conclusion that "the caste composition of the local government leadership does not seem to have significantly changed. The two powerful land-owning castes dominate as in the past while the non-dominant, backward castes have been able to maintain their strength, however insignificant compared to their shares in the State's population. When, however, the totality of the resources which generally make up the political capacity of an Adhyaksha (chairman) is considered, the hold of the major castes in the governance of the Zilla Parishads is likely to be enormous".[4] However, the experience in West Bengal is very different where, in the 1989 Panchayat elections, a lot of people belonging to the landless and deprived sections of society have been elected to different Panchayati Raj institutions and especially to Gram Panchayats.[5]

Would a third tier at the district level, inclusive of sub-district units, enhance the oppressive power of the dominant groups and correspondingly place further burdens on the oppressed weaker sections? Under the present dispensation, it is the dominant groups that hold power at the State level (at least in most States, if not all) and it is largely their writ that runs at and below the district level. The view that high-minded bureaucracy may act as brakes or moderators may be true here and there, but is essentially divorced from reality.[6] Democratic decentralisation to a third tier would not, therefore, worsen matters. Since the logic of democracy favours numbers, one can hope that decentralised democracy would possibly open up opportunities for the oppressed majority to organise itself and capture power at least in a few districts or mandals. Though the organisation of the poor remains a pious and unrealisable hope, it will remain so, as long as the poor have to organise themselves across an entire State before exercising power. By extending the idea of democratically elected governments to the States and stopping there, the system will always remain loaded against the poor and the dispossessed. Carrying the idea down to lower levels would perhaps correct this imbalance.

The ideal of democratic decentralisation, in any case, primarily visualises local government institutions as the primary units of a democratic polity. The fact that they can be used as instruments of socio-economic development can only be secondary. Further, in many parts of India, the backward classes are becoming increasingly aware of the political power conferred on them by adult franchise and there are marked shifts in the inter-caste power structure already. The fear of convergence between the socio-economic structure in a society and the political structure need not, therefore, be overplayed as an argument against either democracy or decentralisation. Undoubtedly there is need for vigilance in this regard, equally as there is a need for policy action in other areas designed to tackle socio-economic inequalities.

Another possible step could be to create appropriate mechanisms that would compel an elected representative to face his constituency periodically and explain to them what he had done and what he proposes to do. It is in this context that the Gram Sabha (or the village council) assumes importance. It should be made obligatory that the chairman and the members of the Gram Panchayat (or the Village Committee) report their work periodically to the council – as is the case in China. The council must consist of the entire electorate in the village (or at least one representative from each household, in case the village is quite big) and shall meet at least twice a year. Problems involving the interests of the entire village shall be submitted by the Village Committee to the council for decision after discussion.

Though such Gram Sabhas are in existence in Karnataka, and will now get established everywhere in India, following the Constitution (73rd Amendment) Act, 1992, they appear to be the weakest link in the chain. The meetings of the Gram Sabha in Karnataka were convened by the Mandal Panchayats at their convenience and in a majority of cases the statutory stipulation of holding a meeting at least once in six months was not adhered to. With an indeterminate agenda and unstructured functions, attendance at the Gram Sabha meetings was not encouraging. It is, therefore, necessary to strengthen this institution and make it the very bedrock of Panchayati Raj. It may be of interest to mention here that in China, as well as in some north-eastern States in India, the villagers' council is vested with the power to dismiss members of the Village Committee and elect new members in their places,[7] and the 1989 Nigerian Constitution contains a provision of recall of an elected councillor by his constituency.[8] Such a power should perhaps be given to the Gram Sabhas all over, to make the elected representative accountable and the people's participation meaningful.

A closely related question is whether there should be separate urban and rural local bodies as in India or a composite local government as in Nigeria. The rationale for parallel systems of urban and rural local self-government could be that the character of the two communities being different, the problems to be managed by these local bodies are altogether different. The rural areas depend on primary production activities whereas the urban areas thrive on secondary and tertiary activities. The land and resource use issues are entirely different and hence it would be desirable to let each system concentrate on issues specific to the character of the communities served. Another argument could be that the fusion of these two types of government might put rural areas to disadvantage. The low level of education, lack of experience in public affairs, inability to control the mass media, the bureaucratic biases, the difficulties in the way of organisation and mobilisation of public support scattered in thousands of small village communities and the capabilities of urban representatives to push through large projects with an urban bias may work against the interests of the rural sector, whereas the parallel systems would insulate and protect rural interests against urban influences. The urban areas, being the main contributors of resources for public investment, might feel a similar threat of being overwhelmed by resource-hungry poor majorities from rural areas.

The costs of parallel forms of local government are, however, equally heavy. They have produced artificial resource constraints. Even though urban populations' need for water, land, energy and nutrients is increasing, it has not been able to develop these resources for more equitable sharing simply because these resources are usually located outside their jurisdiction. Nor have the rural areas been able to develop them because of severe financial constraints. Using their control on State power and money power, the urban areas could offer attractive prices and facilities for increasing the rate of resource exploitation without incurring the cost of resource replenishment. Over a period of time, the cumulatve result of the process of over-exploitation has been the impoverishment of environment from where rural areas could get life supports – free fuel, fodder, fruits, timber, renewal of soil nutrients, unpolluted water, etc. The urban local governments have been reluctant to expand services like water supply, electricity, roads and transport, sewerage, etc., to neighbouring villages because the revenue income from the villages is too small to pay for even a fraction of such services. On the other hand, the land scarcity in urban areas has given rise to the problems of proliferation of slum population in unplanned settlements with severe deficiencies in basic civic amenities, forcing the inhabitants to live in dangerously polluted environments and dilapidated structures.

The administrative costs of a dual form of local government are also high. The State of municipal revenues of small and medium towns is so pitiable that most of them have not been able to meet the basic needs of the citizens. On the other hand, the existing rural local government has staff resources which, with marginal adjustments, could be used to look after the municipal needs of their headquarters town which can be developed as the growth centre for both the urban and rural communities.

The case for ending the dualism in local government is thus strong. A single local government can perhaps look after the needs of its urban and rural components with a set of safeguards built into it so as to ensure just development of the entire area. In the Indian context, a population of one million may be a suitable cut-off, however, exceptions may have to be made in respect of larger-size urban settlements, keeping in view their social and economic settings such as the community identities and the hinterland served by the city. Such a district government can also plan for the entire district obviating the need to have a separate planning body (which is usually created outside the PRIs, as has been the case in India now)[9] to coordinate action by various implementing agencies at the district level, including the Zilla Parishads and city/town municipalities.

It has been suggested that at the local government level, political parties should refrain from fighting the elections on a party basis, to maintain a better atmosphere and minimise conflicts which affect the unity of the village. It is also felt that ideological differences between political parties will be meaningful mainly at higher levels, whereas the local bodies are decentralised units mostly for implementation of development programmes accepted by the country/State as a whole. Such a view, to say the least, overlooks the invigorating role of politics as an engine for change. It also deprives the polity of an entry stage for new recruits into politics and a nursery for grooming such entrants for higher responsibilities.

Of the three parallel structures, both in Nigeria and in India – the administrative, local governmental and the party – only the first one is fully developed and properly operational. While attempts are being made periodically to invigorate the local government structure, the state of the party structure is pitiable in India, with most of the major political parties neither holding their organisational elections nor convening their meetings and conventions regularly. Both the political parties in Nigeria are yet to take firm root, as they have been formed only recently and that too by a decree of the military government. Since participatory democracy will become a vibrant reality only when all the three structures articulate simultaneously, there appears to be no option but to let the political parties fight the local elections on their party symbols. One might argue that change in the ruling parties at the State level may produce a very unsettling effect on the local government institutions. But is that not what parliamentary democracy provides for? If the system can survive a change of ruling party at the centre as a result of the general election, it can easily accommodate such changes at the lower levels.

The district/county government must, therefore, be a political entity looking after the totality of district governance and forming a third tier of the polity. The third tier (or should it be called the first tier?) would subsume self-governing units at sub-district levels right down to the Village Committees. This would mean three things. One, the districts (or the local government areas) must find a place in the constitution – in fact the 1989 Nigerian Constitution names each one of the 449 local government areas in the second column of Part I of the First Schedule to the Constitution and the Constitution of the People's Republic of China provides for county/township governments. The Indian Constitution (73rd Amendment) Act, 1992 also provides constitutional status for the Panchayats. Two, elections will have to be held on a party basis (both in Nigeria and India, as they have a multi-party system) periodically, under the supervision of an independent election authority. Three, the introduction of the third tier should not squeeze the other tiers or be seen as attempting to do so.

Consequently, a clear and detailed recording of Centre-State relations as well as State-district relations, extending the federal idea with as clear a set of functions and powers as possible, to be discharged/exercised by each one of the tiers, either independently or in collaboration with others, should be made in the Constitution itself. Though it is absolutely necessary to clearly delineate the organic relation between one tier and the other, so as to prevent any possible encroachment or misuse of authority by the higher tier on the lower one at a later date, it is a moot point as to whether such a delineation is feasible. While there is no difficulty in making elections mandatory, defining powers and functions and inter-governmental relationships in the Constitution may pose practical problems. Firstly, most of the functions may be overlapping between the State and the local governments. Secondly, even within a country, all the States may not be ready for decentralisation in the same measure. For instance, even if one were to leave out those States in India where there are law and order problems, is the socio-economic environment in, say, Bihar or Madhya Pradesh conducive to decentralisation to the same extent as in Karnataka or Gujarat? The constitutional provisions will, therefore, have to be necessarily general in nature, providing for a reasonably effective third tier of government to start with, covering the essentials, with ample scope for gradual improvement, depending upon the socio-economic settings of the individual States.

It is sometimes argued that since the process of decentralisation is essentially meant for promoting the welfare of the people, not only the different tiers of the structure should have specific responsibilities with reference to development but the higher tier should also own the responsibility of ensuring that the lower tiers do function with a sense of responsibility. For instance, if the Village/Mandal Panchayat passes a resolution which is unjust, unlawful or improper, there has to be a forum of redressal for the aggrieved citizen. Most of the existing Panchayat Acts in India do give such a power, not to an elected body but to a senior bureaucrat of the State Government, usually the District Collector or the Divisional Commissioner. Whether the power to suspend the execution of a resolution or order and/or direct the performance of a particular function by the lower tiers in the decentralised set-up be given to any authority in the first place and, if so, should such an authority be vested in the next higher tier or given to an independent judicial/administrative body is a debatable point.

Once the ZP is recognised as a district government under the Constitution, the relationship between the ZP and the State Government should have to bear some resemblance to the relationship between the State and Central Governments. If the Constitution of the country does not give the Central Government any power to suspend or direct any action of the State Government, then it would be natural to expect a similar relationship between the State and the ZPs. Though the same logic will have to be extended between the ZPs and the lower tiers below the district level, it is possible to argue that the ZPs be given some supervisory responsibilities over the other tiers whose creation and operation may not be governed either by the Constitution or even by a central statute. While it would be proper to leave this to the discretion of the State, suffice it to say that if at all such a power is to be vested with the ZP then it must be exercised either by the ZP or its standing committee and not by a bureaucrat, acting on his own.

In the Karnataka Act, the ZPs have been empowered to dissolve a Mandal Panchayat if it exceeds or abuses its powers or is not competent to perform or makes persistent default in the performance of duties imposed on it under the Act. There is, however, a provision of appeal to the State Government against such an order passed by the ZPs. Similarly, in the case of a ZP, the Government can supersede it on similar grounds.[10] The Act prescribes a procedure providing for the issue of a notice and also a hearing before resorting to such dissolution by the ZP/State Government. One view is that such provisions are necessary to preserve and protect the unity and integrity of the structure, especially in a democracy where the Constitution gives the Central Government powers to dismiss a recalcitrant State Government and impose its direct rule. The other view is that as a rule supersessions should be barred, as it would give the Central/State Governments a handle to remove inconvenient State/District Governments.

Possibility of misuse cannot be an argument against the provision itself. While supersessions should not be resorted to unless in a grave emergency, the absence of such a provision will prevent action even in a genuine case. The possible safeguards one can suggest against any misuse could be: (a) to vest the power of supersession in the next higher tier (and not delegating it to the chairman or to a standing committee or to a senior bureaucrat); (b) to insist on a prescribed procedure which can assure natural justice; and (c) to hold elections in respect of such dissolved body within six months from the date of its dissolution, as the people are the ultimate judges whose verdict should be final. (Such safeguards were in fact provided in the Karnataka Act and, during their entire term of five years, no Panchayati Raj institution was superseded in Karnataka despite political differences between the State Government and some ZPs).

If the local governments are to be distinct political entities, should each one of them be independently elected from a distinct constituency or should there be a link in memberships? Obviously the lowest tier in any system – whether it is a Gram Panchayat or a Mandal Panchayat or the local government area in Nigeria – has to be directly elected. Depending upon the needs of each country, adequate reservations for women/weaker sections may have to be provided, even though such a representation may not be a sufficient condition for their effective participation. Whether there should be single-member or multi-member constituencies and what should be the system of rotation for reserved seats are all details that can be best left to the convenience and ingenuity of the States concerned.

However, the question whether the members of the State Legislature/Parliament (MLAs/MLCs/MPs) should be made ex-officio members of the ZPs is often debated in India. Despite the Ashok Mehta Committee not favouring the association of MLAs, MLCs and MPs with the district-level institutions, both in Karnataka and in West Bengal, they were full-fledged members with a right to participate and vote in the ZPs whereas, in a few other States, they were associate members without any voting rights. The Constitution (73rd Amendment) Act, 1992 leaves it to the State Legislatures in India to decide whether MLAs, MLCs and MPs should be members of the intermediate and district level Panchayats, but, in the event of their being made ex-officio members of these Panchayats, gives them voting rights in all matters except in the election of the chairperson.

The case for involving MLAs/MLCs/MPs in the district-level local bodies for the time being appears strong. Firstly, even though in theory, Parliament, State Assembly and ZP may be independent political entities with a well-defined set of powers and functions, one has to bear in mind the basic fact that all these institutions are to perform complementary roles to each other in the process of development. The question of locating a secondary school or a primary health clinic is a matter of interest not only to the members of the ZP or the intermediate level Panchayat but also to the members of the higher level organs. In a decentralised system of planning, the lower tier assumes as much importance as the higher ones and they should not obviously work at cross purposes. The presence of MLAs/MLCs/MPs in the ZP would help in the planning process and possibly in better fund allocation. The other argument is political. Admittedly, most of the MLAs/MLCs/MPs who are already in positions of power would not like to part with their clout in favour of a new breed of public men who would be elected to various Panchayati Raj institutions. If the nascent local government institutions are to survive the onslaught of influential local-level politicians, the best way would be to keep the MLAs/MLCs/MPs inside the system rather than facing them outside, at least until the system takes root. As an interim measure, perhaps, the MLAs/MLCs/MPs may have to be associated with the ZPs as full-fledged members.

In the middle level, just below the district, the election pattern varies widely. While some States have entirely nominated bodies, some have direct elections and some others get the members elected indirectly. The Constitution (73rd Amendment) Act, 1992 makes direct election of members mandatory at all levels in India. As long as the elections are held simultaneously for all the Panchayati Raj institutions, these direct elections may not be a major burden, either on the administrative machinery or on the State's exchequer. However, keeping in view the fact that this intermediate tier, wherever it exists, would have to essentially perform a coordinating role between the district and the village(s), it may be desirable to ensure that all the elcted members belonging to the lower tier as well as the next higher tier get an opportunity to articulate their views across the table in this forum, at least on a rotation basis.

An interesting feature of the Nigerian Constitution is the educational qualification prescribed for election as a Local Government Councillor – he has to be educated up to at least the school certificate level or its equivalent.[11] It is doubtful whether such a stipulation would stand the test of law in a democracy whose Constitution guarantees the right of equality. That apart, whether formal education should be a pre-condition to hold any public elective office is by itself a debatable point. There are a number of instances where totally uneducated Chief Ministers have distinguished themselves as competent administrators in India.[12] More recently, while describing the initial resistance of rural administration to the Panchayati Raj institutions, Mr Biplab Dasgupta said : "Some derided the Panchayat leaders on the ground that, unlike them, they were not educated. One might actually take this as a positive feature of the present Panchayats in West Bengal that the number of graduates is so few amongst them, indicating its democratic base in a country whose overwhelming majority of people are indeed illiterate. On the other hand, despite their lack of formal education, most elected members are highly intelligent individuals, and what they lack in terms of education is more than made up by their enthusiasm and concern for their own locality as also the detailed knowledge regarding local environment, cropping pattern and people. Besides, they are of proven leadership material, who can motivate people."[13]

Since the elected bodies, by virtue of their size, will not be able to transact their day-to-day business effectively, most of the important matters will have to be settled by the local government executives. Two systems are available at present in this respect. One is the Nigerian model, where the Chairman of the Local Government area (and his running mate, the Vice-Chairman) is elected directly by the people and he appoints three to five supervisory councillors from among the elected Local Government Councillors within 30 days of taking office, and allocates them suitable portfolios.[14] The other model practised in most Indian States has an indirectly elected chairman (from among the elected members), assisted by a number of standing committees dealing with different subjects whose members are chosen on the basis of proportional representation from among the members of the local body.[15] Though both the systems appear suitable for the transaction of business, each has its own advantages and defects.

The average population to be served by a local government in Nigeria varies from 150,000 to 800,000 and in India the population to be served by most ZPs would exceed a million. If a chairman has to be elected directly by the people, the cost of such an election is bound to be high, as the voting population is large and the cost of communication is heavy. While this would straight away preclude the rural middle class/weaker sections from the contest, even the rural rich will be tempted to make good the expenditure incurred in the elections while in office. Though a direct election would assure the incumbent of a tenure in office, such a tenure need not be pleasant or fruitful if the opposition gets a majority in the local government council/ZP. Further, if the local government institutions are to provide a base for a democratic structure, the party system must necessarily extend to the local government institutions and it would be proper to leave it to the party enjoying a majority in the institution to elect the chairman. While there may not be any objections to the direct election of the chairman of a comparatively smaller body, like the Village Panchayat, it would be desirable to prescribe an indirect election for the chairmanship of a larger body immediately below the State, even though in a parliamentary form of government such a chairman has always to depend on a majority support. This is what, incidentally, the Indian Constitution now provides for.

Though the committee system in a presidential model and the cabinet system in a parliamentary model are usually prescribed, it works just the opposite in the case of local government institutions in Nigeria and India. While the directly elected chairman in Nigeria is assisted by a "cabinet" of supervisory councillors, his Indian counterpart functions through a set of standing committees. Every one of the committees that had gone into the working of the Panchayati Raj institutions in India have recommended the committee system without exception, largely to ensure representation to all sections and shades of opinion in a participatory system of development. While the "councillors" are chosen by an individual, namely the chairman, the "committees" are chosen by the entire ZP. Secondly, the decisions would be taken by an individual, namely, the "councillor", in the former system, whereas the latter will have the benefit of collective decision-making.

One major disadvantage with the committee system is perhaps the feeling, especially among the officials, that a major part of their time is lost in attending meetings, preventing them from remaining in close touch with the field. It may perhaps be necessary for each State to decide on the optimum number of committees in a local government and the subjects to be covered by each of them in such a manner that every subject would get the required attention within the least possible time. The Nigerian concept of not letting any local government have more than six departments in all can be usefully adapted to Indian conditions as well. In addition, the role of the committee chairmen vis-a-vis the chairman of the ZP has to be clearly delineated to avoid the possibility of a conflict between the two. This can perhaps be done by evolving a set of business rules or rules of procedure covering the different functionaries of the local government (as in the case of most Central/State Governments all over) – if one does not have the patience to wait for healthy conventions to evolve.

The Maharashtra Act has a curious provision restricting the term of office of the President and the Vice-President of the ZP to two (i.e. 12 years). Such a provision is worth emulating (and could perhaps be extended to the other tiers of the structure as well, so as to break the possible hold of any vested interests in those institutions) if the Panchayati Raj institutions are to properly perform their role of being a training ground for higher responsibilities.

To secure speedy and inexpensive justice in civil and criminal matters of a relatively minor nature, the Karnataka Act envisaged the establishment of Nyaya Panchayats (or judicial councils) consisting of five members (of whom not less than three will have to be from the weaker sections of society, including women) elected in accordance with the system of proportional representation by single transferable vote by the Mandal Panchayat concerned.[16] One of the important functions discharged by a Village Committee/neighbourhood committee in China is to mediate disputes among villagers/citizens.[17] Though there is no "Nyaya Panchayat" in West Bengal, it is reported that people do come to the Panchayat leaders to settle disputes.[18] However, the Ashok Mehta Committee felt that "Nyaya Panchayats should be kept as separate bodies and should not be mixed with the people elected for development panchayats. The members of development panchayats wield executive powers and there are chances that justice may suffer if the two functions are combined".[19] It recommended that the elected Nyaya Panchayats should serve in an area other than that from which they have been elected.

The purpose behind the re-creation of Nyaya Panchayats (which were in existence even before the days of the British rule) is essentially the need to shorten the span between crime and punishment, and injury and redress, as well as the hope that truth would surface locally without elaborate evidentiary procedures. The institution of Nyaya Panchayats will be a valuable aid to the development of social habits of self-government and rule of law. Electing Nyaya Panchayats in a caste and community-ridden society may pose problems in the first instance. In such an event, Nyaya Panchayats could be entrusted with the functions of mediation and conciliation to start with. Over a period of time and with experience gained, a workable system could be evolved combining the local wisdom and the required legal talent.

The process of decentralisation cannot be static. Many of the schemes and functions allocated to a particular tier at one point of time may have to be transferred to a lower tier for better performance at a different point of time. Disputes can arise in the performance of certain functions either within the local government structure or between the local and State/Central Governments. The Dasuki Committee, set up to review the local government administration in Nigeria, in fact recommends for the establishment of an agency to oversee inter-governmental relationships in Nigeria, with particular reference to functions and finance.[20] Such safeguards appear necessary, at least during the initial years of any local government experiment. Both the National and State Development Councils can assume the responsibility for a similar review in the Indian context.

Gandhiji's conception of *swaraj* was "not concentration of authority in a few, but the acquisition of the capacity in the many to regulate authority."[21] In the present political milieu, demand for local governments and strengthening of the local bodies through district governments can even be construed by some as a recipe for disintegration – even though the tendencies of disintegration can be attributed to the fact that neither is there any political power in the hands of the people now, nor is any participation at the local level in decision-making. The least that could be done by any government would be to attempt a genuine decentralisation of power, provide for a vibrant local government structure within the polity in the first instance and allow it to grow, leaving the inter se relationships flexible enough to evolve over a period of time.

NOTES AND REFERENCES

1. *Ashok Mehta Committee Report,* 1978.
2. J. Ayoade, *Area and Administration: Viability Revisited,* University of Lagos Press, 1988, p. 77.
3. The organic law governing village committees of the PRC (trial) adopted by the 23rd meeting of the 6th NPC standing committee on 24-11-1987, article 1.
4. Amal Ray and Jayalakshmi Kumpatla, "Zilla Parishad presidents in Karnataka", *Economic and Political Weekly,* October 17-24, 1987.
5. Biplap Dasgupta, "Panchayatiraj in West Bengal", *Kurukshetra,* February, 1989.
6. Nirmal Mukarji, "Decentralisation below the State level", *Economic and Political Weekly,* March 4, 1989.
7. The organic law of the PRC, *op. cit.*, article 11.
8. *The Constitution of the Federal Republic of Nigeria,* 1989, Section 304.
9. Article 243ZD of the Constitution of India, which has been inserted now, by the Constitution (74th Amendment) Act, 1992, envisages a District Planning Committee to consolidate the plans prepared by the Panchayats and Municipalities within the district.
10. The Karnataka Zilla Parishads, Taluk Panchayat Samitis, Mandal Panchayats and Nyaya Panchyats Act, 1983. Section 271.
11. Nigerian Constitution, 1989, *op. cit.*, Section 299.
12. For instance, Sri K. Kamaraj, a suceessful Chief Minister of the south Indian State of Tamil Nadu for almost a decade never had any formal education.
13. Biplab Dasgupta, *op. cit.*
14. Nigerian Constitution 1989, *op. cit.*, sections 290, 291 and 302.
15. For instance, Section 177 of the Karnataka Act, *op. cit.*
16. Karnataka Act, *op. cit.*, Section 212.
17. The organic law of the PRC, *op. cit.* Article 2.
18. Biplab Dasgupta, *op. cit.*
19. *Ashok Mehta Committee Report, op. cit.*
20. Report of the local government review committee under the chairmanship of Alhaji Ibrahim Dasuki, 1984.
21. Gandhiji, *Young India,* 29-1-1925.

7

POWERS AND FUNCTIONS

The functions devolved upon the local government institutions being highly location specific, exhaustive lists of functions, for any country, will not have much of an operational relevance. Local priorities in all development programmes vary from region to region, even within a country, and it is, therefore, necessary that the individual States have adequate scope for evolving their own list of functional priorities. But this should not mean that decentralization can be viewed as a political charity or administrative concession from the higher to the lower tiers. It is in this context that an irreducible minimum set of functions need to be assigned to the district government and the levels below, leaving open any periodic adjustments that may become necessary in the dynamic process of development, to suit the changing requirements.

There can be two ways of identifying such functions. One is the principle adopted by Nigeria in its local government reforms, namely, to locate the functions which require detailed local knowledge for efficient performance; in which success depends on community responsiveness and participation; which are of a personal nature requiring provision, close to where the affected individuals live and in which significant use of discretion or understanding of individuals is needed, provided such services can be efficiently rendered on the scale of a local government area.[1] On this basis, one set of functions have been listed as items which are the exclusive responsibility of the local governments save in exceptional or temporary circumstances. Along side this list, another set of functions have also been enumerated as local government responsibilities, although State Governments and other organisations may also perform part or whole of these functions if the local governments are not equipped to perform them initially.[2] Prominent among the first list are provision and management of public conveniences, slaughter houses, grazing grounds, etc., most of which can be grouped under "provisions of local services", and collection of local taxes. The second list includes the key subjects of health, education, agriculture, water supply, sewerage, etc. The general theme of distribution appears to be to hand over to the local governments such functions which they need to discharge (and which cannot be discharged by the distant State Government) and leave the rest flexible.

The other method is the Gandhian principle of Swaraj or what is called in modern management jargon "management by exception".[3] This implies what the village or Village Panchayat can do for itself should not be done by the authority at a higher level. What the Zilla Parishad can do for its area should not be burdened on the State Government. Likewise, what the State Governments can do, with regard to their constitutional responsibilities, should not be loaded on the Central Government. In this system of rationalisation, every unit from the smallest to the largest is made to do the maximum it can, without unnecessary dependence on an outside authority. The question, therefore, is to identify the maximum set of functions which can be suitably and efficiently managed by the local government institutions, leave it to them entirely and distribute the resources accordingly. This method would be more in tune with the concept of democratic decentralisation as, in a democracy, the people are sovereign and, therefore, distribution of power should be from the base upwards. That is to say, the Village Panchayat should first determine what powers it should keep for itself for the purpose of administration and development of the village and the residuary powers only will be delegated to the other levels. The district and State Governments should also decide likewise.

Though in theory the latter principle should be ideal, in practice it could become extremely difficult to achieve, at least until the local government system takes root and grows into a position of strength from where it can demand its rightful share. Until then, the allocation of functions has to be on the basis of local conditions and mutual negotiations.

Anyway there is an agreement, by and large, in most part of the world that proper managemant of resources like land, water, forests, grazing grounds for the animals, etc., require local-level planning. These will, therefore, have to be brought under the local government set-up. Second important function relates to efficient landuse programmes, so that the needs of food, fodder and fuel can be met locally as far as possible. Third function could be the provision of basic minimum needs such as primary education, adult literacy, primary health care including child health and family planning, drinking water, rural roads and efficient functioning of public distribution system.

Experience in India has shown that where the primary schools are under the control or supervision of locally elected Panchayats, the attendance of teachers has improved enormously whereas in other areas, there are instances where primary teachers have been drawing their salary without even showing up at the centres and in some cases even auctioning their jobs to others at a lower price.[4] Similarly, attendance of the medical staff had improved tremendously where the local Panchayats have been supervising the health centres. The strict enforcement of family planning in China is largely attributed to the influence and control exercised by the village and neighbourhood committees, who have been given the responsibilitiy.[5] The reason for all these is simple. The local people have a stake in getting education for their children and health care for their families. So they insist upon the presence of these functionaries at their assigned posts. In a centralized system of direction and control from above, these functionaries do not feel the need to make their full contribution.

One more function relates to the village industry and anti-poverty programmes, both of which need an intimate local knowledge to be successful. The township and village enterprises in China numbering 18,686,300 employing 93,667,800 persons with a gross output value of 742,838 million yuans ($140 b) per annum are all being managed by the local bodies concerned.[6] In some cases, the township governments have taken prompt action to improve the efficiency and profitability of operations of their enterprises, as it would have a direct impact on their financial position, which in turn would be crucial for the efficient discharge of their own functions. This may not perhaps be possible under other political systems wherein the market forces play a major role in determining pricing. Though the local governments in these systems may not themselves take on the task of running village and small industries, they can at least encourage the growth of these industries, by creating the necessary infrastructure and environment. Finally the district government will have to have its own set of regulatory functions also such as maintenance of land records, registration of birth, death and marriages, collection of local taxes, etc., which has an impact on local administration and development.

Rural Safety

The question of whether rural safety should also be given over to the control of the local bodies, more particularly the district governments, needs some attention. A distressing feature of the Indian rural scene in the past decade has been a determined effort by the privileged groups to put down the underprivileged by resorting to extreme violence and cruelty, especially against the scheduled castes and backward classes who seek to free themselves from social injustice and exploitation that has gone on for decades. A relatively large number of incidence of such violence has been reported from Uttar Pradesh, Madhya Pradesh, Bihar, Rajasthan, Maharashtra and more recently even from Gujarat and Tamil Nadu. According to the 1991 Census, around 74.3% of the Indian population, or over 628 million live in 579,000 villages, half of which are situated in difficult terrain characterised by poor socio-economic conditions. In a country like India, where about three-fourths of her population reside in the villages, ensuring peace and security only in cities and towns inhabitated by just one-fourth of the population, is hardly conducive to the progress and prosperity of the nation as a whole. The situation in Nigeria or China is not very different either. No government, State or Central, can afford the huge costs involved in deploying a regular police force for guarding each and every village of the country. The problem of rural safety, therefore, requires a different approach and re-orientation to ensure adequate protection of life and property of the rural poor.

The system of village headman, assisted by one or more village watchmen for policing self-sufficient ancient villages, was in vogue in India, well before the Vedic days. Even the British, who destroyed many local institutions that existed in India for ages, consciously retained this system of rural policing, with minor alterations.[7] Under the East India Company, the village police agency was made primarily responsible for watch and ward of the area within the jurisdiction, for notifying the nearby police station of suspicious activity, commission of crime or public unrest and to assist the regular police in the maintenance of law and order and investigation of crimes. This system was allowed to fade away and was replaced by a chain of police stations and outposts, after the dawn of independence. Since the beginning of this century, all the police commissions/committees set up in India have accepted the impossibility of carrying on an efficient rural policing system by means of official policemen and have stressed the need to secure the aid of the village community in that endeavour. If that be so, why not make use of the Panchayats which represent the local people?

Unfortunately the police administration and the reformers of police have also abhorred the idea of linking police organization with Panchayati Raj.[8] Their main apprehension has been that those bodies consist of individuals involved in petty jealousies and factional politics and would not be able to discharge these functions in an impartial manner. They also believe that, given the socio-economic inequality and the fact that the power structure at different levels is controlled by the dominant castes, it may be unsafe to entrust police administration to the local government institutions. This argument has been successfully adopted by the ruling elite at the State level (who in any case beleive that their writ will not run, in the rural areas, without the coercive arm of the police) without realizing for a moment that the same could be advanced against some State Governments as well. When social pattern in the countryside is undergoing a radical change through the establishment of local governments, the other administrative and executive institutions functioning in the area will also have to undergo a corresponding change, sooner or later, to fit in with the changing pattern of rural administration. The elected representatives of the people who constitute the Village Panchayats are the most appropriate instruments of the government, for the maintenance of public order and policing in their own areas. The process of democratic decentralization cannot be complete, without the gradual transfer of the functions and powers of the village police from the State Government officials in the village to the Village Panchayats. In most of the developed countries, policing is a municipal job and there is no reason why it should not be so in India, Nigeria or China.

Decentralised Planning

The entrustment of development functions to local institutions would remain incomplete unless these institutions are vested with the authority to take their own decisions and plan according to their own requirements. Planning would, therefore, be an important function to be discharged by all the tiers of the local government structure. Unfortunately this has not been so in any of the three countries – Nigeria, China and India. At least in China, there was a system of local planning during the days of the communes. The planning process began during the middle of each year; commune proposals incorporating the needs and priorities of the production brigades and teams and taking cognizance of available manpower and financial resources were passed.

on to the county; after discussions with communes, the county passed on the total production targets and demands for inputs to the province, for onward transmission to the central planning commission; after the annual meeting with provincial representatives to review and refix targets and making suitable adjustments thereafter, production targets and priorities were passed back to the lower levels in the form of guidelines with the "basic needs" approach to development.

The Chinese communes played a key role in identifying new industrial possibilities, examining market prospects and supplying investment funds and technical know-how for implementation.[9] Though there was no composite plan for the development of the area, at least a production plan was prepared in every commune. With the advent of "household responsibility system" and the disappearance of the communes, the concept of local-level planning in a formal sense is no longer discussed in China as, in their present system, the local governments have become essentially implementing bodies under the guidance of the higher level bodies. The word "planning" does not even find a place in their 1987 Village Committee law.

The Nigerian system, however, accepts the concept of local level planning and casts it as a duty on the local government to participate in economic planning and development of the area, but pleads its inability to implement it in right earnest, putting the blame on the acute shortage of funds and lack of skilled manpower to take up local planning.[10] The experience in India is not very different either. Though the Second Five Year Plan had laid down, as early as in 1956; that each village would prepare a production programme and the services required at the village level, all the village plans will then be embedded coherently in a block plan, and likewise block plans in district plans leading up to State and national levels, the pity is that this excellent methodology was never enforced.[11] The reasons for this are both historical and political.

Historically, central planning and administration were considered necessary to guide and control the economy and to integrate and unify the nations that were emerging from long periods of colonial rule. It was believed that central planning and industrial investments concentrated in a few major metropolitan centres would "trickle down" and spread throughout the economy to alleviate poverty and generate income and employment at the sub-national levels. The capital mobilised through savings would be re-invested, thereby expanding production and employment, raising income, drawing large number of people into productive process and eventually pushing the poor into a stage of self-sustaining economic growth. Regional disparity would gradually be lessened and the majority of the people would benefit from the continued growth and development.

But, by the end of the 1960s, it was widely recognised that central planning had not achieved these goals in any of the developing countries. The economic growth remained sluggish and even where the growth rates were high, only a small group usually benefited from the increased national production. Income disparities between rich and poor and among regions varied. The living standards of the poor had declined and the number of people living in absolute poverty in the rural sector increased.

Many development planners and administrators began questioning the effectiveness of strategies based primarily on central planning framework aiming at increased industrial output and challenged the existing theories of economic development. The Planning Commission in India then came up with the twin proposals of "growth with social justice" and "decentralized planning" to reorganise the growth pattern. A working group was set up in September 1982, "to define the precise scope and content of district planning; to delineate the procedure for decentralised planning at the State level to make the concept of district plan optional and to devise the various steps in district planning and indicate methodologies for each step".[12] The report of this working group which was submitted in May 1984, besides detailing the methodology of district planning, recommended an organisational framework consisting of district planning bodies in which the District Collector will play the role of the chief coordinator. The report made no mention of the Panchayati Raj institutions either as a prerequisite for district planning or as an institutional mechanism to undertake local level planning.[13]

The political reasons for centralised planning are obvious. Firstly, it would be increasingly difficult to take major investment decisions having political dimensions in a decentralised set-up. Secondly, the ever increasing central schemes and centrally sponsored schemes, which many a time are used to distribute political patronage especially during an election year, will run into difficulties with decentralised planning. For instance, even after the introduction of decentralised planning process in Karnataka (which will be described later in this chapter) a review undertaken by the Government of Karnataka revealed that in the year 1988-89, the Zilla Parishads had freedom to spend only 14 per cent of the total plan outlay and the rest of the money had been "committed" by the Central and State Governments on various new/ongoing schemes sponsored by them.[14] With little political commitment, the planning machinery at the State level in most parts of India was kept weak, not to speak of the district level; the data-base was weak, development administration was never geared to the task and the institutional mechanism in most districts was totally absent.

Though the advent of ZPs in Maharashtra and Gujarat had brought the concept of district planning into the local bodies, over a period of time, the planning responsibility was taken away from the ZPs and entrusted to the independent district planning bodies under the chairmanship of a State Government Minister, with the District Collector playing the key role in plan formulation. Even to this day, except in Karnataka, where district planning is an essential responsibility cast on the ZPs, the other States in India have their district plans formulated either by an independent body outside the ZP or through the bureaucratic arm of the District Collector. This makes the Karnataka model worth narrating.

The Karnataka system provides for planning right from the village level. Though it is the Gram Sabha (i.e. the village council) which is expected to prepare and promote the development scheme of the village in its open meetings, in actual practice what really comes out of such meetings is a list of demands, prominent among them being a school building, drinking water supply, primary health centre, veterinary dispensary and a link road to the nearest market centre. These demand lists are considered at the next higher level, i.e., by the Mandal Panchayats (which consist of a group of villages) and a sub-plan for the Mandal is then prepared accommodating the requirements of individual villages as far as possible. The Taluk Panchayat Samiti, at the Block level, which is mostly an advisory body, reviews the Mandal plans within the Block, and passes them on to the ZP at the district level, with its comments. All the Mandal plans are scrutinized by the planning cell of the ZP, which then prepares a district plan for the consideration of the ZP, which is the final planning and implementation authority in the district. This process has been designed to ensure that, in some way or the other, every local aspiration, even at the village level, is taken note of.

Under the existing planning process in India, State Plans are finalised by the national Planning Commission before they are budgetted. State's draft plan has to be sent to the national Planning

Commission usually in October or November every year. Since the State Plan has to be built upon the plan proposals of all the ZPs, the plan exercise at the ZP level should begin earlier than the State level. In order to facilitate this, a tentative allocation has to be intimated to each ZP (and in turn to the Mandal Panchayats) against which the ZPs formulate their plan proposals for the next year. For this purpose Karnataka had decided to adopt a tentative reasonable outlay for the State even before the planning commission holds resource discussions with the State.[15] The following "planning calendar" was, therefore, prescribed for adoption by the State and local bodies in Karnataka[16] :

July 15	Adopting the tentative size for the State's Annual Plan for the next year beginning April 1.
July 25	State Government's Planning Department indicates to the ZPs and Mandal Panchayats the financial ceiling within which their annual plan should be formulated for the next year.
August 15	Mandal Panchayats to send their plan proposals to ZPs, after convening Gram Sabhas in each of the villages within their jurisdiction.
September 20	ZPs to send their draft District Plan to the State Planning Department and the other concerned heads of the departments in the State Government.
September 28 to October 25	Discussion with individual ZPs on their draft Plans by the State Planning department for achieving consistency and integration of district sector with State sector schemes/plans.
November 10	Government/State heads of the departments to consolidate these proposals and build them into the State's draft plan and send the same to the national Planning Commission.
January 15	Approval of the planning commission to the State's plan, after discussion with the State representatives.
February 25	Finalizing the State's plan budget in the light of the Planning Commission's approval to the State Plan and finalizing the district plans of the ZPs accordingly.
March 10	Presentation of the State's budget to legislature along with the link document giving schemewise, sector-wise and ZP-wise outlays.

The most noteworthy part of the whole exercise was the active participation not only by the Gram Sabhas but also by the ZP Presidents, who, without exception, opted to lead their district's delegation in the discussions with the State Planning Department, setting aside strict protocol – they held the rank of a Minister of State, whereas the State team was always headed by the State's Planning Commissioner, a career bureaucrat usually.

For realising the objective of regional balance through decentralised planning, Karnataka had adopted a certain criteria for distribution of Plan outlays among the ZPs, giving a relatively higher share to the backward areas/regions. These have been summarised in Table 7.1.

TABLE 7.1: Indicators and Weightages for Distribution of Plan Outlay

Indicators	Weights (%)
1. Population	50
2. Backwardness in agriculture as measured by the value of agricultural output per hectare.	5
3. Backwardness in Irrigation as measured by the proportion of Irrigated Area to Net Area Sown.	7
4. Backwardness as measured by the value of Industrial Output.	5
5. Backwardness in Communications as measured by Road and Railway mileage per 100 sq.km and per lakh of population.	5
6. Backwardness in Financial Infrastructure as measured by size of population served by each commercial and cooperative bank.	2
7. Backwardness in Medical and Health Facilities as measured by the number of hospitals per 1000 population/bed population ratio.	5
8. Backwardness in Power Supply as measured by the proportion of villages electrified.	5
9. Problems of the Weaker Sections:	
a) as measured by the proportion of SCs/STs in the population;	2
b) as measured by the proportion of Landless Agricultural Labourers.	2
10. Special Problems of Malnad areas and Drought Prone Areas:	
a) as measured by the area under forest;	2
b) as measured by the rural population of Drought Prone areas.	2
11. Literacy Percentage	5
12. Performance in Family Planning Programme	3
TOTAL	100

While this would take care of the allocation of Plan funds among the ZPs on an equitable basis giving weightage to backward districts, similar criteria needs to be fixed for determining the share of the Mandal Panchayats within the ZPs (based on the schemes to be transferred to the Mandal Panchayats) which in turn will have to be spent within the Mandals. For this purpose, the following criteria had been adopted.[17]

Indicators	*Weights (%)*
1. Population	50
2. Area of Mandal	15
3. Dryland Area	15
4. Agricultural Labour Population	10
5. Per Capita Resources Raised	10

A 10 per cent weightage to resources raised by Mandals was given keeping in view the need to encourage Mandals who perform better in mobilising the resources. Similar indicator was not included for ZPs since they did not have taxation powers. These criteria were to be adopted until the Finance Commission for ZPs and Mandal Panchayats constituted under the Karnataka Act, suggests a formula for allocating funds to the local bodies and the State Government takes a decision on it.

The system of decentralised planning described above is likely to be continued, even under the three-tier system of panchayats to be established under the new Karnataka Panchayat Raj Act 1993, with necessary modifications to suit the three-tier structure. The Constitution (73rd Amendment) Act, 1992 also envisages the preparation of plans for economic development and social justice as one activity that should be legitimately entrusted to the panchayats. It is, therefore, necessary to look at the experience gained, while implementing decentralised planning, during the five years of its operation in Karnataka through the erstwhile panchayats.

Though the state government had decided to assign a free outlay in the form of lump sum allocation for ZPs and Mandal panchayats for formulating their own development plans, there have been some difficulties in achieving the same. First is the possibility of different ZPs adopting different norms for the implementation of identical or similar schemes. In any case, no deviation from the prescribed norms are possible in the case of central sector and centrally-sponsored schemes under the present guidelines issued by the Planning Commission. Secondly, schemes like Minimum Needs Programmes which carry 'earmarked outlays' are being implemented by the ZPs and Mandals. So long as there is conformity between the lower tiers of the government and the State Government as regards the priorities of such schemes, there may not be any problem. But conflicts can arise if their perspectives differ. In order to avoid any such possible conflict, it may have to be necessary to earmark outlays for these schemes – as is being done in the National Planning Commission, while approving the state plans. Taking these factors into consideration, Karnataka chose to earmark outlays from the lump sum allocations made to the ZPs and Mandals, keeping such earmarking to the barest minimum possible (mostly to the schemes identified by the National Planning Commission for such earmarking). Table 7.2 summarises the actual planning process that was carried out in Karnataka during 1988-89.

An analysis of the 1988-89 annual plan indicates that the ZPs gave priority for social services followed by rural development programmes, agriculture and allied services and communications. Among social services, ZPs allocated higher outlays for primary and secondary education and rural water supply. Within these sectors, the emphasis was on appointment of teachers and construction of school buildings and class-rooms and piped water supply respectively. While the allocation for roads and bridges was increased substantially, in sectors like animal husbandry, particularly for opening of rural veterinary dispensaries and mobile veterinary clinics, the outlay was doubled, when compared with that of 1987-88, the plan for which year was prepared by the state bureaucracy.[18]

Even after the issue of such detailed procedure, some grey areas still remained. The Karnataka Act stipulated that the ZPs and Mandals could reappropriate funds from one service to another, subject to a maximum of 10 per cent of the budget. Many ZPs felt that this restricts their freedom. Secondly, the local governments should have their authority and responsibility to modify or discontinue an existing scheme transferred to them to ensure a proper use of available resources. While such a step could be taken straightaway by the State Government in relation to the State Plan schemes, it had to persuade the Central Government/National Planning Commission to follow a similar course in relation to the centrally sponsored schemes – which was not only difficult but also time-consuming.

Thirdly, decentralised planning brings into focus the need to obtain information from and dissemination of knowledge to a large number of local bodies. For the efficient execution of national schemes with national priorities, it is necessary that the flow of information from one tier to the other is smooth and timely. With the existing level of managerial skills and a not too reliable communication network, colleciton of data from the decentralised institutions and a possible mid-course correction on that basis was virtually impossible.

TABLE 7.2: Planning Process in Karnataka (Illustration of 1988-89 Plan)

State Plan Outlay (provisionally fixed at Rs.1000 crores)	
State Sector Rs.756 crs	ZP Sector Rs 244 crs
	Government communicates outlay of ZP and Mandals and asks ZPs to prepare composite district plans (JULY).
Distribution among departments and finalisation of sectoral allocations (OCTOBER)	ZP distributes outlay to each Mandal based on criteria (AUGUST)
	Mandals hold Gram Sabhas, finalise their plans and send to ZPs (AUGUST)
	ZP prepares district plan by integrating Mandal plans with own plan and sends to Government (SEPTEMBER).
	Government level meetings with each ZP, attended by Heads of Departments, to finalise the plans (OCTOBER).
Sectoral outlays of State and district plans integrated in each department, and State Plan finalised (NOVEMBER)	
Draft State Plan discussed with Planning Commission and finalised for an outlay of Rs 900 crs (JANUARY)	
Outlays in State sector (Rs.660.69 crs) and ZP Sector (Rs 239.31 crs) revised and incorporated in the State Budget (FEB -- MARCH)	
Approved outlays communicated to the ZPs (MARCH)	

Fourthly, the most important problem that came into sharp focus was how to reconcile the process of decentralisation with a comprehensive national planning. In any country, the need for planning arises primarily because of the fact that in relation to the requirements of economic development, the financial resources which the country can mobilise are inadequate and what there is, should be utilised optimally to reach the desired socio-economic goals. Prioritisation at the national level, therefore, becomes a necessity. As long as the priorities of the nation and the felt needs of the local people converge, there will be no difficulty in decentralised planning. Otherwise, it can create endless problems, resulting at least in delay if not in the breakdown of the process. For instance, the Planning Commission would be fully justified in insisting on earmarking of funds for "social forestry", to augment the country's dwindling forest resources, whereas the local Mandal would like to assign a very low priority for social forestry, in its scheme of things. In other words, there is an inherent dichotomy between the freedom which should be available to the PRIs and the discipline demanded by national planning. In practice there has to be a compromise between the two.

These problems in decentralised planning are not entirely unanticipated. In any dynamic process of development involving several partners, the occurrence of such problems only indicate the health of the system. The best way to evolve acceptable solutions is through frank discussions between the different tiers which the system itself provides for and by public debates, involving planners and practitioners even outside the system. There is also no need for solutions across the board applicable to all the States/Provinces, as the process of planning is indeed intended to bring out better utilisation of the limited resources in a given area.

Unfortunately, development planning is still undertaken, in many countries, under very stringent data constraints. Relevant demographic data, educational data, rural resources data, household data and other socio-economic data, basic to effective planning are either lacking or are grossly unreliable.[19] Local governments are at present almost entirely left out of the process of data collection (with the possible exception of the collection of demographic data) even though they are ideally located, to collect and maintain spatially comprehensive database for planning and other day-to-day operational objectives. There is, therefore, a need to strengthen the local governments to function as grass-root units for data collection as well. In addition, since planning implies harmonisation of resources – internal and external as well as financial and human – with needs, the local governments, at the district level at least, should have adequate technical expertise to assist the elected representatives in local-level planning. This was singularly lacking in Karnataka.

Regulatory Functions

In a district government set-up, it will not be possible to compartmentalise "regulatory" and "development" functions, as each has repercussions on the other. For instance, a successful implementation of land reforms would ensure that the Panchayats are not dominated by big land owners, as has been the case in West Bengal. Sometimes a minor irrigation project may require the aquisition of land from the people and their consequent rahabilitation. It would, therefore, be necessary to have the regulatory land revenue function very much within the ambit of a local government; so will be the case with the distribution of essential commodities, organisation of regulated markets for commodities, etc. However, the emphasis should be on local governments being meaningful agents of development and they must, therefore, play an effective role in the fields of agriculture, rural development and diversification of the rural economy, by engaging in the development of rural industries, rural transportation and a wider range of other rural social amenities.

Rural Development and People's Participation

As the State and Central Governments neither have an easy and direct access to rural population, nor are they directly accountable to the people at the grassroot level, the local government structure seems to be ideally suitable for rural development. Moreover, "many in the administration feel that the official machinery by itself is not suitable for carrying out the development programmes which call for a great deal of initiative and participation on the part of the people themselves".[20] Though the people's participation has been the subject of popularity without much clarity, a somewhat closer description could be "voice in the selection of the scheme, role in executing it and partaking in the fruits of development".[21] If that be so, locally elected organisations should be the obvious choice through which public participation can be channelised.

However, there are also reservations about the role of local governments in rural development through the people's participation, which arise from a widely shared view that the weaker sections of the rural community may not feel that their interests will be fully protected by these institutions. There is also an extreme view in India that "the leadership of the PRIs acts as a "gate-keeper" and prevents the flow of benefits to the weaker sections of the rural community".[22] In their opinion, bureaucracy was considered a better option. Contrary to prevalent myth, the development administration is more solidly allied with the rural rich than the much maligned local bodies of the past. The combination of the rural rich and the bureaucracy is formidable. The alienation of the people from the most exciting task of development, on the one hand, and the continuation of the colonial pattern of administration – directed from the top and unaccountable to the local population – on the other, have serious implications for both development and democracy, both in the short and long term.[23]

Local governments, which are subject to periodic changes through the electoral process, are at least becoming increasingly more sensitive to the pressures of the poor. For all its faults, the institution of elected governments offers the best hope for development with equity, economy and integrity in the absence of any other option in sight. It opens the door for the weak, to influence the development process and, over time, the poor can even gain control of at least a few local governments in a country.[24]

Keeping in view the distinct advantages in utilizing local government institutions as vehicles for rural development, it is possible to think of at least three safegaurds to ensure their effectiveness and equity. First is to implement the agrarian reforms legislations (ceilings and tenancies) which are on the books, but which are successfully bypassed and eroded. With a skewed distribution of rural assets – in India the bottom 39 per cent of rural households own five per cent of all assets, while the top five per cent own 46 per cent – it will take a very long time for the rural poor to raise their voice. Second is to strengthen the village council, i.e. Gram Sabha. It is only at this level, and at no other level, that all the adult people can directly participate and suggest what can and need be done for their own village and how. At all other levels, people have to be substituted by "leaders", elected or otherwise. Only a strong village council, whose meetings must be convened by the chairman of the Gram Panchayat periodically as a part of his statutory duties, can ensure "the acquisition of the capacity in the many to regulate authority".[25] Third is to create an environment where local initiative and voluntarism can grow and to establish linkages which would produce a new partnership between the local governments and the non-governmental organisations for progressive rural development. The voluntary agencies can play an effective role as catalysts to educate the people on their rights and duties, organise them to participate in development activities, encourage them to participate in elections as voters and candidates and help them to act as watchdogs to prevent any misuse or corrupt practice. They can also induce or force functionaries to guarantee social justice to the weaker sections.

In the ultimate analysis, true development is the development of the people and this can be fostered only by creating institutional structures which are commanded by the people, which are responsive to their needs and aspirations, and which put instruments of development in the hands of the people. In this sense, district governments, which combine in themselves the regulatory and developmental functions, need to be strengthened so as to provide a strong base for any democracy.

NOTES AND REFERENCES

1. *Guidelines for local government reform,* 1976, Government Printer, Kaduna, para 4.
2. *Ibid.*, para 5, table I.
3. Interview with L.C. Jain, "Panchayati Raj and decentralisation", *Kurukshetra,* February 1989.
4. *Challenge of Education*, Ministry of Education, Government of India, 1987.
5. In China, it is the Village Committee that maintains the details of eligible couples within the village and tells them when to have their child. Any violation leads to imposition of penalties.
6. *China statistical year book*, 1990.
7. Sitaram Singh, "Panchayatiraj and rural safety", *Kurukshetra*, March 1989.
8. *Ibid.*
9. S.A. Olanrewaju, *Local government and economic development in Nigeria,* University of Lagos Press, 1988, p. 204.
10. My discussions with Mr. E.A.O. Oyeyipo, Deputy Governor of Kwara State on 9th Oct., 1990.
11. Interview with L.C. Jain, *Kurukshetra, op. cit.*, 1987.
12. Government of India, Planning Commission, Office Memorandum No.PC (P) 35/1/82-MLP dated 22nd September, 1982.
13. *Report of the working group on district planning*, Government of India, Planning Commission, May 1984.
14. *Karnataka shows the way, district governments and decentralised planning,* Government of Karnataka Publication, 1988, p. 45.

15. *Proceedings of the Government of Karnataka*, G.O. No. PD3 PRN86 dated 19th December, 1986, para 14.
16. *Ibid.*
17. *Ibid.*, para 11.
18. M. Sankaranarayanan and M. Basavanna Goud, "Status of district planning in Karnataka", *Paper* presented in the seminar on district planning organised by the Indian institute of management, Bangalore. 1989.
19. S.A. Olanrewaju, *op. cit.*, p. 216.
20. T.N. Chaturvedi, "Democratic perspective in administration", *Prashasnika*, 3(3), 1974, p. 31.
21. Kuruganty R. Sastry and C.P. Vithal, "Participatory dimension in rural development: The case of Panchayatiraj", *Journal of Rural Development*, NIRD, Hyderabad. Vol 7 (6), 1988.
22. Report of the working group on block level planning, Government of India, Planning Commission, 1978, Chapter 6.
23. L.C. Jain, *Gross without roots*, Sage publications, New Delhi, 1985.
24. *Ibid.*
25. Gandhiji, *Young India*, 29th January, 1925.

8

FINANCIAL AND HUMAN RESOURCES

Before we get on to discussing the financial resources of the local government, which should take precedence over a discussion on its human resources, it may be necessary to have a look at the economic justification for local government, as conventional wisdom on local government usually glorifies only the political justification. For example, the earliest justification for local government was provided by John Stuart Mill who justified local government in a democracy as an institutional safeguard against concentration of power with the Central Government and that it would provide an appropriate training ground for political leadership.[1] However, the economic justification for local government and local fiscal system never got widely appreciated.

The economic case for local government has been developed by a few eminent economists[2] on the basis of the need to achieve efficient allocation of resources placed at the disposal of the public sector. Provision for certain public goods like security of life and property is considered essential for the very existence of a society. It is generally felt that the market mechanism fails to supply optimum levels of these public goods in view of the failure of the citizens to reveal their preferences for such goods. Therefore, in a democracy, the government is expected to provide these essential public goods.[3] The government is expected to step in when the market fails to efficiently allocate the society's resources. This is the economic justification for government. The emergence or creation of government as a collective institution is justified for the supply of public goods which are essential for a society. These include protection of life and property, maintenance of law and order, etc.

There are several types of public and "merit goods", i.e. goods which "merit" government assuming at least partial responsibility for their supply without requiring the citizens to pay for them as they are socially important, such as primary education, public health, etc. Some of them, like defence, involve economies of scale in their provision.

Some other public goods have to be spatially restricted for achieving efficiency in their supply. Since efficient provision of optimum levels of public and merit goods at least unit cost requires meeting the demand for such public services according to the varying tastes and preferences of the citizens, the need for spatial delimitation of the provision of various types of public and merit goods arises. This need for spatial delimitation of supply of public goods justifies multi-level governments in a democracy – Central, State and Local.[4]

There is an economic basis for allocating functions and sources of revenue as well among these multi-level governments. Some public goods, which have a wider spatial coverage and which involve economies of scale in their supply, will have to be provided only by a national-level government. Since these essential public goods are to be made equally available to all citizens free of cost, their costs have to be met by compulsory levies like taxation at the national level. Similarly, some other public and merit goods, which have limited spatial coverage and which have to be catered to varying tastes and preferences, become the responsibility of the State and local governments. Though the most efficient way to finance these types of public and merit goods is to raise funds, linking every public good to a corresponding financing proposal, such a trading of public goods for voluntary payment may not always be possible, especially in a developing country. This justifies the need for local taxation.

Some taxes involve economies of scale in administration. Such taxes will have to go to the Central or State Government. Others which have only a local base and which require local knowledge for administration come to the local governments. But such taxes tend to yield less revenue than the taxes which have a nation- or State-wise base, thereby a situation would invariably arise where the local govenments are left with inadequate revenues for supplying local public and merit goods. Consequently, financial transfers from the higher-level governments to local governments become necessary to meet their requirements to provide certain essential local public services (which need to be provided only by them to ensure efficiency in supply). This is the justification for Federal-State financial assistance to local governments.[5]

However, one may argue that, if the Central and State Governments raise the revenues for the local governments to spend, the vicious principle of "financial irresponsibility" would develop, i.e. if the higher-level government raises most of the revenue for the local governments to spend, it will encourage them to become extravagant because they do not face the problem of raising revenue and hence facing the political consequences of reckless spending and heavy taxation. It may also be argued that too much dependence of the local governments on the higher-level governments for finances would impair the financial sovereignty and expenditure responsibility. But it is also true that the very existence of higher-level governments with constitutionally allocated sources of revenue limits the scope for raising substantial revenue at the local government level, particularly when the local governments are the creatures of the State Legislatures. Secondly, even though it may be possible to allocate an equal number of functions and sources of revenue to the local governments, it is a practical impossibility to estimate either the exact cost of each function or each source of revenue and to match both. Thirdly, these functions being very basic and essential to society, expenditure on them cannot be adjusted to the level of revenue in a year of poor or uneven receipts. Therefore, the ideal principle of absolute financial independence is a practical impossibility. What can be done at best to prevent a possible wastage of natural resources placed in the hands of the local government (feared by those who believe in the principle of "financial irresponsibility") is to make at least a few financial transfers conditional and to provide for administrative and audit checks on spending. This is the justification for all the Central/State sponsored schemes and budgetary releases and controls for specific sectors and schemes to the local governments.

Thus, if the principle of allocative efficiency is used for justifying the creation of local governments and also for assigning them with local functions and financial resources, a situation would arise where they have to depend on both internal and external resources to meet their obligations. If the local governments are to have a semblence of fiscal autonomy, it is obvious that their own revenues should amount to around half of their total revenue receipts. Though this would be an ideal situation for a local government to function, in reality it seldom happens.

The local governments are thus left with only four types of resources in (a) local taxes, (b) user fees, (c) subsidies and grants from higher levels of government, and (d) loans. Local taxes and user fees are collected from the people (and enterprises) living in the local government jurisdiction. They can be described as resources mobilised domestically, as against grants and loans which are generally mobilised outside the jurisdiction. A local tax is generally a tax whose base and rate are determined by the local government, its collection is undertaken by the local government and its proceeds accrue to the local government. A user fee is a fee paid in exchange for a service provided by the local government. A fee is voluntary (one only needs not to buy a service in order not to pay the fee), whereas a tax is compulsory. A fee is utilised to finance the particular service for which it is levied, whereas a tax goes, in principle, to the general budget. A fee is independent of income, whereas a tax is generally based on ability to pay. In reality, these differences are often blurred. The consumption of some of the services for which fees are charged is in practice unavoidable, so that these fees are very much like taxes. Some taxes are earmarked and utilised to fund specific services, just like user charges. Some user fees vary with income, just like taxes. Similarly the distinction between subsidies and loans can also be vague, as the terms of some loans may include an element of subsidy.

How should a local government decide on the taxes and fees it can mobilise locally? The financial requirements of a local government depend on two things: (a) the type and variety of the functions it is expected to perform, and (b) the extent to which any given function is to be performed within the period of time relevant to the concerned financial flow. The former is conditioned by the degree of decentralisation, i.e. if a State chooses to delegate to the local governments only a few functions, it may be that the financial resources they get, though small, are adequate for discharging these functions. The problem in that case is not one of inadequacy of financial resources, but of the limited vision underlying the scheme of "democratic decentralisation" of that State. The latter depends on the prioritisation of activities within the local sector set out in the State's plan and also by the degree of maintenance required to keep assets/services in a reasonably good shape to ensure the continuous performance in a satisfactory manner of the relevant activities of the local sector. Since planning should be the key function that must be assigned to the local governments, it should be possible for them to assess at the beginning of each year their requirements for the year and plan how much they need to collect through local tax and user fees.

What are the taxation powers that should be given to the local government to meet this financial obligation? While it is absurd to have a standard list for all countries or for all States within a country, the experience gained in different countries does indicate a common set of taxes such as property tax, income tax, business tax, etc., that are usually levied by the local governments. Property taxes are taxes based on the value of properties owned by households and enterprises. Their importance varies from country to country, but in many countries, both developed and developing, property taxation is the main form of local taxation.[6]

As a local tax, the property tax has many desirable features. It is, to a large extent, borne by the people who live in the jurisdiction in which it is levied. The tax on land is borne by landowners, most of whom live in the area. The tax on residential/commercial structures is borne by the occupants, whether they are tenants or owners. The tax is fair in the sense that the people who bear the burden of the tax will benefit from the expenditures financed by the tax. Secondly, the property tax does not reduce or prevent production. It does not affect the land supply or an existing structure, as no one would reduce the land or demolish a structure in order to escape taxation. Thirdly, the tax is progressive as its incidence is usually relatable to wealth/income. Finally, the property tax is buoyant. Even at a constant tax rate it will produce a growing tax yield since the tax base, viz. the value of the land and buildings is growing. Despite these advantages, the property tax in most developing countries has been proved to be difficult to administer, mainly due to three types of leakages – incomplete coverage, insufficient or inaccurate valuation and inadequate collection.

An additional difficulty is that, in a developing country, many properties are of very small value. Yet the cost of taxing a piece of property is largely independent of the value of the property and of its potential tax yield. This means that for many properties the tax cost will be as high as or higher than the tax yield. A logical solution might then appear to be to exempt low-value properties from taxation. But the cost of identifying low-value properties is the bulk of the cost of taxing them! In addition, exempting some properties will set an example and pattern for other properties; it might also be unfair if someone who owns one large property is taxed whereas someone else who owns several small properties of a larger total value is not taxed. Despite these difficulties, property tax will have to continue as the key source of internal revenue for most local governments.

Local taxes on income are rare, particularly in developing countries. Though the tax can be progressive, here again administrative difficulties are great. Assessing the income of individuals or households is generally beyond the capabilities of most local governments, even in the developed countries. The taxes on local business are no better. Besides providing a large scope for evasion, they may also have the fair chance of being passed on to the consumer, which will in the long run harm production itself. Thus the accrual to the local government exchequer through the source of local taxation does not seem to be impressive, strengthening the general impression that the efficiency of tax administration cannot be as high as when a tax is administered by a higher-level government which is insulated from latent tax payer discontent. Though an individual tax payer may believe that he is not getting the proportionate benefit from the governments at any level – especially when he is faced with deteriorating public services such as inadequate water supply, absence of public toilets, etc. – the intensity of it is more at local government level. Hence any allocation of resources to local governments will have to take into account this fiscal psychology of the residents at local government level. A heavy reliance on user fees to augment local government resources could be useful, but that again would depend on the quality of service provided.

Whatever may be the difficulties in mobilisation, local governments have a duty to generate their own local resources, for at least three important reasons. Firstly, it gives them a sense of autonomy and also financial responsibility. Secondly, it gives the local people a sense of participation through their own resources in the process of development at the local level. Thirdly, it changes the equation between the local and State Governments – from that of a beneficiary-donor relationship to the level of at least unequal partners in development. The real problem is, therefore, to select the appropriate types of taxes and fees, taking into consideration different and often contradictory administrative, economic, social and political constraints. No mix of taxes and fees will ever be perfect. The local governments should, therefore, be prepared to constantly review and improve their internal mobilisation systems.

The system followed in China to ensure financial autonomy for local governments needs to be mentioned here. The financial resources available to local governments in China are not determined by the number of taxes they levy, but by the number of enterprises they control. They can increase the production quota of any or all of their enterprises or they can form new enterprises making use of locally available raw material. It is their control over the tax base (and not on the taxes per se) that gives a sense of fiscal autonomy to local governments in China. Besides this method, there is yet another option available for Nigerian and Indian Governments – which is by vesting public assets such as forests, public lands, fishery tanks, quarries, etc., in the appropriate local governments so that they can maximise the income out of these resources through efficient and concentrated management and augment their internal revenues.

External resources – borrowing and inter-governmental grants – clearly have an important role to play in financing local governments. While borrowing – whether through intermediaries or from the Central Government – is essential to finance major capital investments/productive assets, it can neither be an assured source of finance nor can it be recurring. Borrowing has to be on a case-to-case basis and that too for an income-generating asset, which can perhaps pay back the entire loan over a period of time. The local government may let any of its enterprises borrow and stand guarantee for repayment (as is done in China) or borrow directly and request the higher-level governments to stand guarantee if the financial institutions were to insist upon it (as is the case in India).

The methods adopted for inter-governmental grants in Nigeria, China and India vary considerably and provide for a very interesting comparison. In Nigeria, both the national local government reforms (1976) and the Constitution (1989) provide for a grant-in-aid from the Federal and State Governments to the local government. At present, while the federal government has to grant 15 per cent of its revenue, each State is required to pay 10 per cent of their internally generated revenue to the local governments. (These percentages are prescribed by the National Assembly from time to time.) The exact distribution of grants among the local governments varies from State to State; but it is usually based on population, land area and equality. Unfortunately the dependence of the local governments on this grant-in-aid is excessive. There have been instances wherein the delay in releases (or the non-release sometimes) had adversely affected the execution of works in individual local governments.

Under the Karnataka model, the Zilla Parishads do not have any taxation powers and are, therefore, dependent on the release of funds by the State Government. (Though the Mandal Panchayats had powers to levy local taxes, their internal revenue was insignificant in most cases.) To ensure that the releases are not left entirely to the mercy of the State Government, two safeguards have been provided in the system. Firstly, funds are allocated to the Zilla Parishads, on the basis of demands voted by the State Legislature. Each department, while presenting its budget before the State Assembly, separately indicates the district sector schemes which are to be implemented by the Zilla Parishads in a link document and gets approval for the release of necessary funds. Secondly, the releases are not made by individual departments to the Zilla Parishads, but by the State finance department once a month, taking into consideration the voted demands and the budgets of the Zilla Parishads concerned. The important point, however, is that the allocation of funds from the Central and State Governments is on the basis of a formula through which the Plan funds are allocated and not on the basis of any fixed percentage of the internally generated revenue of the respective government.

A unique feature of the Karnataka model was that it provides for the appointment of a State Finance Commission to recommend:[7] (a) the pattern of assistance; and (b) the principles which should govern the grant-in-aid from the State Government to the Zilla Parishads. Though the first term of reference implies that the commission should recommend whether the State Government should provide financial assistance in the form of tax shares, grant-in-aid, loans or in all these forms, the second term leads one to believe that the intention appears to be to maintain a donor-beneficiary relationship between the two governments.

This is in marked contrast to the provision in Article 280 of the Constitution of India, under which the States are entitled to a share of the resources raised by the Union by virtue of their being the federating units in a common union. The net proceeds of the taxes mentioned in Article 280 constitute a common pool of resources from which the Centre and the States draw their shares as determined by the National Finance Commission. Though the intention of the Constitution makers was that the financial transfers should be mostly regulated by the awards of the Finance Commissions, they did provide for grants from the Union to certain States (Article 275) with an operational flexibility (Article 282), to meet possible contingencies. Unfortunately, in practice, the system got so distorted that the resource flow under Article 282 is now in excess of the statutory transfers as per the Finance Commission awards. Learning from this experience, perhaps, the Karntaka Act provides only for the flow of assistance and grants-in-aid from the State Government to the ZPs. A more fitting basis for financial relations between the State Government and the Panchayats has been envisaged under the Constitution (73rd Amendment) Act, 1992 by redefining the scope of the Finance Commission which now includes making recommendations as to the principles which should govern the distribution between the State and the Panchayats of the net proceeds of taxes, duties, etc., leviable by the State and the allocation between the Panchayats at all levels of their respective shares of such proceeds (Art 243-I).

In China, the local governments receive very little grants from the Central Government and there is no regular pattern of inter-governmental grants either. The strength of their fiscal system lies in the mode of tax-sharing. The provincial and local taxes in China are indeed central taxes, as the tax rates and bases are set centrally. But, unlike most countries, the taxes are collected not by the Central or Provincial Governments, but by the local governments and shared up to the higher levels. The Central Government determines that a specified share of all taxes collected in each Province is passed on to it, taking into consideration the fiscal capacity and the expenditure needs. The variation across the provinces is wide, indicating the affluence or poverty of the region. Similarly the Provinces decide the tax-sharing ratios between the Province and individual local governments, without any Central Government approval. The shares are decided well in advance, so as to give an adequate incentive for the local governments to collect the taxes.

From the points of view of fiscal autonomy as well as the costs of tax collection, the Chinese model appears to be the best. However, it suffers from some serious defects such as no clear segregation of tax sources between the Centre and the Provinces, no stability in sharing of resources and the near total dominance by the Centre in the decision-making process. It is a part of an authoritarian system and may not exactly fit into a democratic set-up. Still local governments in other developing countries can adapt this model in the limited sphere of tax collection and fiscal autonomy to their advantage. Even the political consequences of such an adaptation may not be much, as the revenues from exports and such other centrally controlled operations can still be substantial in a developing country, to ensure a constant flow of funds to Central and State Governments. However, the political situation in most countries may not permit such a quantum jump in the near future. The next best option could be to constitutionally assure a percentage or quantum of internally generated revenues to be passed on as inter-governmental grants to local governments so that the latter can plan for its utilisation every year. If the local government lacks adequate expertise to plan for itself, as is generally held in Nigeria, Central/State Governments can at best indicate a sample basket of schemes that could be implemented and leave it to the local governments to choose appropriate schemes depending on their own needs and priorities. Such a step would assuage the present feeling of local governments that the development programmes are generally imposed from above, howsoever complete the process of consultation between the State and local governments may be.

Human Resources

The three countries present an interesting variation in the utilisation and development of human resources as well. Since the local governments are integral parts of the system and the human resources are jointly owned by all the levels of government in these countries, a look at the administrative systems practised in these countries in the first place becomes imperative.

The Chinese administration is characterised by a structural fusion, with the administrative hierarchy paralleled by and intertwined with the party hierarchy. This has solidified the ruling party's control over the State bureaucracy. Soon after Deng Xiaoping came to power, in the wake of Mao Zedong's death, he raised the issue of administrative reform as an important means of achieving the nation's modernisation. In October 1978, he pointed out that modernisation calls for many changes "in the relationship of production, the superstructure and the forms of management in industrial and agricultural enterprises, as well as changes in the State administration over these enterprises".[8] Deng's administrative reform featured three themes – professionalisation, market regulation and rule of law, aiming at reduction in bureaucratic control over resources and a possible downfall in the importance of government officials in society.

Bureaucracy is known for its resistance to change and this becomes even more obvious when the change involves bureaucratic machinery. As Anthony Downs observed, "All officials tend to oppose changes that (a) cause a net reduction in the amount of resources under their own control and (b) decrease the number, scope or relative importance of the social functions entrusted to them".[9] Though the opposition of the Chinese bureaucracy to the proposed reforms was, therefore, understandable, two factors came in the way of their opposition. First, the party maintains a tight control over the State bureaucracy. Through numerous party branches penetrating the administrative structure, the Chinese Communist Party has ensured an administration obedient to its political boss. Second, previous political campaigns have left an indelible impression on brueaucrats' minds. To oppose the party and its policies has meant an ignominious end for one's career (and life). In the interest of their own survival, the Chinese bureaucracy had, therefore, to "adjust" themselves to the reforms. Though some authors believe that this adjustment is negative, serving the cadre's own interests rather than the goals of reform,[10] there is enough evidence to point out a closer involvement of the bureaucracy in all levels of government, following the reforms.

Professionalisation in China was designed to make administrators more competent in order to facilitate modernisation. At the outset of the reform, only four per cent (about 1.6 million) of party members were college educated and approximately 10 per cent were illiterate. Only six per cent of the 810,000 leading cadres at various levels of State institutions, party and mass organisations, enterprises, etc., had college education. Approximately 11 per cent of the county leaders, 14 per cent of the bureau heads in provinces and 20 per cent of the provincial leaders had college backgrounds. Although China is an agricultural country only a paltry 3.6 per cent of the leading cadres in charge of agriculture at provincial and county levels had formal training in agriculture.[11] Though the details of the professionalisation are not available, a number of scattered reports, however, indicate that substantial progress has been achieved, through the reforms, on the goal of promoting younger and better educated persons than before.[12] However the attempt to separate government from direct economic management, designed to prevent administrative interference in economic activities, led instead to thousands of new companies run by government agencies and officials. Rules banning the cadre's involvement in commercial business were so belated and ineffective that many of these companies remained alive and well, at the end of 1988.[13]

Though a Communist regime cannot afford to break up its dual hierarchy for the sake of administrative reforms and better economic management, the indications are that this would be attempted to the extent possible and increasing reliance would be placed on the system of examination and evaluation introduced by the Central Committee in 1982. The factors to be judged in these evaluations are political consciousness (*de*), ability (*neng*), diligence (*qiu*) and physical condition (*ti*).[14] Cadre allocation below the provincial level is expected to continue with the provincial leadership and the administrative cadres to be sent to the rural areas will invariably be decided at the county level.

Faith in the ruling party's political ideology is bound to be the common thread that would run through the different levels of government in China.

On the contrary, both Nigeria and India have inherited the British legacy which is based on the Weberian model of national-legal bureaucracy, implying that all decisions are to be taken objectively according to clearly laid down rules and procedures. The major foundations of the British model of the administrative system were policy-implementation (and party-government) separation, public accountability, civil service neutrality and rule of law. A key element of the colonial system was the district administration – the prefect-like omnipotent figure at local level, appointed by the central or regional government. While this was entirely abolished in Nigeria, following the local government reforms in 1976, it still continues practically everywhere in India.

Many observers, mostly academicians, felt strongly that the post-independence administration in both these countries would have to change its character drastically. They saw a distinct dichotomy between the colonial and developmental bureaucracy. The new administrator should be one who emphasised results rather than procedures, teamwork rather than hierarchy and status, flexibility and decentralisation rather than control and authority. He should be outgoing and people-oriented. In brief, they felt that the traits and styles required of a new bureaucrat were those of a manager of a business enterprise.[15] The colonial style of bureaucracy was thus to be thrown out. But, this did not happen. On the contrary, the top-level national leadership, at the time of independence, in both these countries, which were considerably socialised to the Western culture and which had some experience of managing organisations, put their faith in the system they had inherited and opted to utilise the same bureaucracy to attain their developmental goals.

Over three decades of persistence with this system has resulted in the administration being "regarded as having gone from bad to worse and as being wooden and unresponsive, overgrown in size but far from efficient". The citizen finds the so-called cutting edge of administration, which provides his interface with the government, to be blunt and abrasive. If he has a grievance, he does not generally get prompt redressal. What is worse, there is pervasive corruption. The words "bureaucracy" and "bureaucrat" have acquired a pejorative connotation.[16] The extension spirit is very feebly and intermittently articulated in the developmental bureaucracy, causing concern to the national planners. Nor is the rural development bureaucracy accountable, except in fiscal terms – which could easily be made fictitious. As regards accountability to the people, it is still a far cry.

The unsavoury image of administration in both these countries, is not wholly unfounded. Admittedly there has been a growing consciousness among the general public, over the years, of their rights while their expectations have kept widening. But the economic advancement, both in Nigeria and in India, has been so slow that, viewed in terms of improvement in levels of income, employment opportunities, welfare services, etc., there is a general feeling of dissatisfaction and discontentment. The inability of the economy to respond to the rising expectations is, of course, basic to an over-populated, poor country like Nigeria or India. But it is not uncommon to find the administration being denigrated for mismanagement. Secondly, the general deterioration in standards and values, widespread corruption and poor work ethic, which one finds in society today, have also inevitably permeated into the administration. Thirdly, the rising scientific and technical content in a variety of government activities calls for a higher degree of knowledge and skills and a growing need for specialisation which the generalist administrator finds himself ill-equipped to meet.[17]

But there is also a positive side to this picture. There is, even now, a large proportion of honest and dedicated officials in both the countries. In times of crisis, the administration has given a good account of itself. For whatever progress India or Nigeria has achieved, the administration does deserve some credit, because of the important role played by the bureaucracy in a developing country which is yet to develop its fully structured political and social institutions. This apart, persons from different sections of society are now employed by the Central and State Governments (which still remain the largest employers in these countries) and their potential needs to be harnessed. The solution, therefore, cannot be to get rid of the bureaucracy, but to design a proper role for them, equip them for the role so that they are able to respond to changing needs and demands, allow them to perform and hold them accountable.

If the administration is to be responsive, its structure and system have to be functionally appropriate. If changes in the range and type of functions are not paralleled by structural adjustments, strains will inevitably develop in the administration. Paradoxical though it may appear, the people, for whom the programmes are meant, have no control now over programming nor over the bureaucracy which administers these programmes. In such a context, little effort would be directed naturally towards the building of local capabilities and local will. Fortunately it is now being increasingly recognised that administration cannot be a wholly top-down operation and if it is to achieve maximum impact, the involvement of local people at various levels through appropriately designed institutions is necessary. This indeed provides the administrative rationale for the local government system in Nigeria or the Panchayati Raj in India.

If the deterioration in administration has to be arrested, three kinds of measures need to be taken. First, a structural decentralisation of powers and functions to the maximum extent possible and creation of new institutional mechanisms. It is only through the local government institutions that accountability in administration can be improved. It must be clearly understood that an administrative system which is essentially visualised as an instrument, and had indeed been used as an instrument, cannot be a primary "change agent". Both the administrators and the people's representatives must realise this and establish new equilibria, to facilitate development of the people, whom they both serve. Second is the redesign of services, which is perhaps beyond the scope of this book. While generalist cadres might have been adequate for the colonial period where the activities of the government were limited, there is a greater need now for functional services so as to provide specialised cadres to different levels of government. Third is to encourage non-governmental organisations including the cooperatives to take over some of the functions now being discharged by government, specially in the area of welfare. The phenomenal growth in the number of government employees needs to be arrested, if the quality of performance is to be ensured.

While most of what we discussed till now will apply to all levels of government, there are two specific issues to be discussed in the context of human resources in a local government set-up. First is the method of getting proper officials to serve the local governments. The role of a local official differs from that of a central civil servant in several ways. His unit of administration, including policy-making, is much smaller than a national department. It has a shorter history, and the terms of service are often less firmly established. The employer is nearer, and is more involved with the details of the official's work – indeed the employer and the client public are closely linked. Because the work is related to a limited geographical area, "horizontal" links between the technical functions tend to be stronger than in the national service; the local departments need to understand each other's activities from day to day. At the same time there are demands which remain the same for both national and local services – the need for efficient administration, and the need to preserve a flexibility of response. Local officials have to be equal in ability to those doing similar work in the Central Government, and they must be promoted on merit; anything else is a recipe for failure. The difficulty of providing these requirements, while preserving a degree of loyalty to the local unit, has led to experiments with the three types of personnel system,[18] namely:

(a) *Separate*, in which every local authority acts as a completely autonomous employer;
(b) *Integrated*, in which the local authority's executive is composed of central civil servants; and
(c) *Unified*, in which local authority staff are employed locally but organised nationwide in a single civil service, parallel to the central one.

Commonest throughout the world is the *separate* system, which is the natural response to a legal decentralisation of powers. Even here, some common arrangement is needed to support the merit principle and establish a link with standards that apply in the national civil service. This can be done by national laws and regulations, though at some risk of rigidity and a shift towards the actual control of staff by the centre. Or it can be provided by non-government bodies: as in the United Kingdom, there may be associations of the employing local authorities which negotiate at national level with the professional staff associations and trade unions. In either case the object is to produce accepted gradings and terms of service that run throughout the system (with exceptions that can be agreed to suit local conditions). The employee's loyalty is single – to the authority which employs him – but a full career is open to him, whether he stays in one place or moves elsewhere on transfer. Problems arise where local authorities are too poor to pay the staff that they need, or too small to offer them adequate experience in the professional task, or where nepotism prevails in making appointments and promotions. The separate system demands considerable maturity in the local unit.[19]

An opposite solution is the *integrated* system found in countries which have no strong tradition of decentralised government. It offers complete homogeneity and transferability since officials belong to the central civil service: salaries, conditions of service and pension rights are uniform. Staff can be posted wherever they are needed, and the problem of finding sufficient local resources to pay for them does not arise. But the system leads directly to control from the central or the "deconcentrated" offices of government. Annual reports and disciplinary action inevitably bring in the national administration; even minor staff questions are referred upwards, and local flexibility is lost. More seriously, there is a split between loyalties which faces every senior official: his "operational" loyalty to the council, and his "career" loyalty to his central masters. If he has any ambition for his own future, no officer is likely to defend the council's interests where they clash with the ideas of a minister or principal secretary. So the autonomy of decision-making by local representatives is undermined.[20]

The *unified* system is an attempt to escape the snags of the other two systems. Here a separate central body, like the Local Government Service Commission in Nigeria, which is independent of any other State apparatus, comprehensively deals with the senior bureaucracy in the local governments and often serves junior grades to a limited extent as an appellate authority. Its responsibilities include the establishment of a national grading scheme, setting up equivalences with the government service procedures for recruitment, control of the promotion and discipline of senior officials and their transfer from one local authority to the other. The system thus provides for a structured career to the local government bureaucracy and also protects them against any unfair discrimination. At the same time, it encourages loyalty to the local authority, much the same way as the separate system does.[21]

Of the three systems, the separate system needs to be discarded as it generally results in a set of low-paid local employees of low status and poor efficiency with very little scope or incentives to work. It can be applied only to the junior cadres, for whom the attraction of staying back in one place or within a small local government area can be an adequate incentive, besides small promotional opportunities which are within the means of the local government. It can also apply to such cadres which are large enough to provide mobility and promotional opportunities within the cadre. For instance, the number of primary school teachers in each district in India is so large that they can conveniently constitute into separate district cadres.

While the integrated system suffers from the malady of frequent transfers and dual loyalties, the only drawback with the unified system appears to be that it prevents a healthy movement of bureaucracy between the different tiers of government. The experience of the Indian Administrative Service (IAS) needs to be mentioned here. Most of the senior bureaucrats in the Central and State Governments, who are from the IAS, start their career as field officers in the sub-districts and put in substantial years of service in the District/State Governments. This certainly puts them in a more advantageous position than anyone who would work only in one tier of government. It works to the advantage of the State as well. Secondly this mobility between the State and local administration gives them both the experience and the status, to give effective, impartial and practical advice to their political masters. Interestingly even in China, the top bureaucracy at the provincial, county and township levels mostly comes from outside the province, county and township concerned, as they believe that such persons can take impartial decisions on the day-to-day running of the system, even though they are bound by the overall policy directions issued by the local party hierarchy.

While one should prefer the unified system for most part of senior local government administration, it will indeed be desirable to bring in the concept of mobility between different tiers built into the administrative system. The details of how this can be achieved could perhaps be left to the countries concerned, but with two provisos. First, there should be a fixed tenure system, i.e. when one leaves a particular tier of government to serve in another, it should normally be for a specific period (say, three to five years) so that frequent transfers are avoided and both the officer and the system can benefit from each other. Such a practise is prevalent even now in India between the Central and State Governments. Second and perhaps more important is that this mobility should cover all levels of higher bureaucracy – as against the present system of sending juniors in the hierarchy to the districts, with the seniors occupying higher positions in the State and Central bureaucracies (which has in effect "reduced" the effectiveness of the field officers). For instance, a permanent secretary at the State level will have to serve as the chief executive of the district government and vice versa, if society has to reap the full benefit of an integrated administrative structure.

The second issue that has a bearing on the local government system relates to the role of the district officer (or the district collector, as he is called in India). While Nigeria abolished the district officer system in stages after independence, China never had it, even at the time of the proclamation of the People's Republic. Though some authors (mostly the former district officers who later turned academics) in Nigeria believe that, "the district officer was a most vital link between the State Government and the field administration and this link has been broken since his demise. . . . In his local government role of inspection and supervision, the district officer succeeded in many areas in saving many local governments even from themselves... though the institution of the district officer has disappeared from the local government scene, his roles have not disappeared and the gap left behind in the system is yawning",[22] the chances of a re-emergence of the district officer in Nigeria are bleak. So the issue is relevant only in the Indian context.

The institution of Collector in India owes its origin to the East India Company when Waren Hastings in 1772 nominated the erstwhile tax collection supervisors as collectors, investing them with the executive powers of managing revenue collection. When the districts came to be recognised as functional and manageable units of administration in 1778, the Collectors were made the chief district officers responsible for the interpretation and execution of government thinking and policies.[23] The importance of the Collector grew over the next century and by the time the British took over the administration, he had become an identifiable linchpin whose status and authority could not be diminished.

Even after independence, when the Governor-General and Governors of the British India were replaced by democratically elected governments at the Centre and in the States, the districts continued to be administered as before. Even today, barring a very few States in India, the District Collector continues to be the person through whom all the regulatory and developmental functions of the State get discharged. With an elected district government, as an established third tier in the system of governance, what would be the relevance of a District Collector? Viewing it from the opposite angle, would it be wise to dispense with the institution of a District Collector completely, having regard to the linchpin role he has been playing so far? As Nirmal Mukarji puts it, "The)vernors of British province performed a similar role. Their replac ient by elected governments was considered logical and appropriate i ndia's federal democracy. The performance of most of the elected S : Governments leaves much to be desired, but that has not produc a yearning to go back to the governors. Replacing district officers by elected governments could reasonably be expected to follow the same pattern. Besides, today's district officer would be tomorrow's chief secretary of a district government. His administrative powers would then be infused by a political content, due to his proximity to those in power at the district level, and this would increase rather than diminish his role as a coordinator and supervisor".[24]

Though the more recent Karnataka model has also kept the District Collector outside the development administration, which has been entirely handed over to the local bodies, his position needs to be reconsidered, at least in the next phase when the regulatory functions of the State will have to be brought within the ambit of the local governments. His rightful position appears to be that of the Chief Secretary of the local government, with all the other heads of departments assisting him in the implementation of programmes, as members of the local government's management team. Under his leadership, the team can also mobilise all available human resources within the local government area, for instance, teachers and graduates from the colleges, polytechnics, members of women's clubs and youth clubs, etc., so as to involve as much local expertise as possible, in the process of development.

More important than the administrative reforms is the cleansing of the environment. The need to restore a sense of idealism and a spirit of dedication among the elected representatives, bureaucracy and the other sections of society will remain a real challenge in developing countries for a long time to come. Training not only administrators but also elected representatives, in the patterns of social, economic and political relationships could enhance the ability of local governments not only to equip them with the necessary skills for promoting development faster in their areas but also to reduce areas of friction. Nonformal methods can also be used to create awareness, interest and determination among the people for vertical mobility.

NOTES AND REFERENCES

1. J.S. Mill's essay in R.B. McCallum (ed). *Considerations on representative government*, Oxford University Press, London, 1948.
2. For instance, Dr. G. Thimmaiah, in his paper on "Finances of PRIs in Karnataka", Institute of social and economic change, Bangalore, 1986.
3. *Ibid.*
4. Richard M. Brid, *Central-Local Fiscal Relations and the Provisions of Urban Public Services*, Centre for Research on Federal Financial Relations, The Australian National University, Canberra, 1979.

5. Dr. G. Thimmaiah, *op. cit.*
6. Remy Prud'homme, L'oeil, "Internal mobilisation of resources", EDI *policy seminar report.* No. 21, 1989.
7. The Karnataka Zilla Parishads, Taluk Panchayat Samitis, Mandal Panchayats and Nyaya Panchayats Act, 1983, Section 210.
8. Deng Xiaoping, *Selected works of Deng Xiaoping (1974-82)*, Foreign Languages Press, Beijing, 1984, p. 146.
9. Anthony Downs, *Inside Bureaucracy*, Little, Brown & Co., Boston, 1967, p. 274.
10. Stephen K. Ma, "Chinese bureaucracy and post-Mao reforms", *Asian Survey*, Vol. 30, No. 11, November 1990, p. 1052.
11. *Ibid.*, p. 1039.
12. See *Xinhua*, The New China News Agency, 29-3-1983.
13. Stephen K. Ma, *op. cit.*, p. 1050.
14. Thiagarajan Manoharan, "Basic party units and decentralised development", *Copenhagen Papers*, Centre for East and Southeast Asian Studies, Museum Tusculanum Press, 1990.
15. See Anil Bhatt, *The Social and Political Dimensions of Administering Development in India*, 1987.
16. T.R. Satishchandran, "Changing challenges to administrator", *Times of India*, Bangalore. 1-10-1988.
17. *Ibid.*
18. See Philip Mawhood *Local Government in the Third World*, Chapter I.
19. *Ibid.*
20. *Ibid.*
21. *Ibid.*
22. L. Ademolekun, *Local government in West Africa*, University of Lagos Press, 1988.
23. Dr. Sundeep Khanna, *Collector through the centuries*, Government of India Publication, May, 1988.
24. Nirmal Mukarji, "Decentralisation below the State level", *Economic and Political Weekly*, March 4, 1989.

9

CONCLUSION

Developing countries are usually faced with a dilemma on the issue of decentralisation, whether it should be a deconcentration or a devolution. In the first instance, most of them will opt for a devolutionary decentralisation, patterned after their colonial master, wherever there was one. After the initial rhetoric dies down, the system will degenerate and settle down to deconcentration, with creation of parastatals alongside. This was the pattern at least in Nigeria and India.

Three reasons can, of course, be adduced for this situation. First is the problem of political integration. Many countries are far from a Nation-State status at the time of their creation; threats of secession and rebellion are not infrequent from the different ethnic groups/tribes constituting the nation. Wide latitudes of autonomy are, therefore, usually frowned upon by national leaders.[1] Secondly, there are economic arguments highlighting the scarcity of resources to promote decentralisation, which will leave the local governments always in a weak position. Finally even from an organisational point of view, many countries may not be able to provide suitable manpower even to undertake decentralised planning. Many, therefore, believe that while centralisation may lead to stagnation, decentralisation will lead to chaos.

In spite of the vigour with which these arguments have been advanced, equally weighty arguments highlighting popular participation in decision-making, provision of efficient services at the cutting edge, liberty in resource mobilisation, etc., have been pursued by the protagonists of decentralisation. To them, even good government is no substitute for self-government.[2] I will agree with the view that the need for an effective local government system is enhanced or limited by the overall environment of the State itself and the nature of the community should dictate the form of administration that it needs and the degree of responsibility that it should accept.[3] For instance, the system that may work well in a particular Indian State need not work equally well even in a neighbouring State, as the culture and environment of these two States may vastly differ. What is important, therefore, is the need to adapt the system to suit local conditions and aspirations.

Unfortunately, most Central Governments often view local governments in terms of local service delivery only. There is a common joke in Australia that a local government's image is seen in terms of the garbage disposal and control of stray dogs and that council representation reflects these needs.[4] If that is true, then there is little opportunity for communities to become involved in their own development through the media of local governments and the limited range of services can perhaps be administered equally effectively by a few public servants. The role of a district government must be much more than a mere provision of local services. It should be a vital link in the chain of national development. It is a part and parcel of the State apparatus and it provides for an indispensable avenue for integrating and shepherding social demands, which can be used as a powerful instrument of socialisation. Some analysts, therefore, feel that the "local government is important less for the issues it decides than for the issues it keeps submerged".[5]

If that be so, why does the actual implementation of the plans for decentralisation stand in sharp contrast to the proclaimed intentions? What really happens in the field? U.C. Agarwal, a senior civil servant from the Indian Administrative Service, who recently retired as a Permanent Secretary to the Government of India, gives a vivid account of the decline when he narrates:

> Officers of my generation were serving at the district level during the initial period of implementation of the Community Development Programme and the National Extension Services. During this phase, initially there was enthusiasm, mutual cooperation and understanding among the officers and local leaders in translating the Community Development ideology into visible action and in implementing with active popular participation various local development works to satisfy their "felt needs". One of the conditions in implementing all local development works was that the villagers concerned would contribute 25 per cent to 50 per cent of the cost either by way of labour or in cash. At the beginning, there was not much problem in getting voluntary labour as part of the people's contribution for works like village roads, minor irrigation projects, drinking water wells, school buildings, Panchayat Ghars, etc. Com-

> mittees of the local people nominated by the Panchayats and not contractors executed these small works.
>
> Before long, however, the villagers' enthusiasm and contributions disappeared. The local bodies started inflating the estimates to such an extent that a work could be completed with Government grants alone and the balance of the higher cost adjusted as people's contribution. At a later stage, even contractors appeared as nominated leaders of Panchayats to execute these works. This led to an enhancement of the estimates to cover both the people's contribution and the contractor's profit. Instances of fictitious execution of works also started coming to light. Thus the usual ills of bureaucracy like inflating costs, corruption and delay in execution reappeared with the elected local bodies also. Their internal factions, groupism, political rivalries and mutual mud-slinging further obstructed speedy completion of projects. These shortcomings and squabbles caused disappointment and disillusionment with the PRIs. . . .
>
> . . . Village democracy or "gram swaraj" remained more of a romantic dream, the harsh reality being different and distasteful.[6]

"In spite of all this," he conludes "it cannot, however, be said that there were no success stories at all or that the situation could not have been retrieved given more time and necessary political will to guide and nurse the nascent popular bodies." Neither was the Ashok Mehta Committee prepared to view Panchayati Raj as "a god that failed". It noted the following merits:

"(1) Politically, it became a process of democratic seed-drilling in the Indian soil, making an average citizen more conscious of his rights than before.
(2) Administratively, it bridged the gulf between the bureaucratic elite and the people.
(3) Socio-culturally, it generated a new leadership which was not merely relatively young in age but also modernistic and pro-social change in outlook.
(4) From the developmental angle, it helped rural people cultivate a developmental psyche."[7]

An added dimension to the whole situation is the experience of many African countries, where the local governments appear to thrive under a military or unitary regime rather than in a democratic set-up. Does it mean that the military/unitary regime would like to encourage people's participation at lower levels, just to legitimise its stranglehold of power or does it betray the fear of the democratically elected State leaders over the emergence of a new and parallel power structure at a level closer to the people or both? Anyway, democracy in itself is a rather vague concept. It applies in a polity where rules and conventions of the political game are set and operated by the members of the polity through a conscious and active involvement. Without commitment to the rules of the game by the members of the polity, the whole idea of democracy can at best be a mere idealism. In such a situation, how can local government autonomy be ensured in a democratic set-up? These are questions which a political scientist would perhaps be more equipped to handle.

However, from our point of view, if local government is to be regarded as a vehicle for promoting social and economic development, then efforts must be made to improve its image as an effective third tier of government and this must be reflected in the basic constitution of the country. A mandatory provision in the Constitution is sacrosanct, whereas a statutory provision in the State law may not have quite the same sanctity.

While suggesting a constitutional position to the local governments in any country, it is, however, necessary to caution that uniformity and standardisation in the institutionalisation of local governments should not be carried too far, if it is to take on a good deal of local character–though there are certain essentials which need to be mentioned, so as to make the identity and integrity of the local governments reasonably and substantially inviolate.[8] For instance, the essence of democracy is elections. There must, therefore, be a provision to ensure regular and periodic elections to local governments. Similarly a provision has to be made for ending the sickness of unending suspensions and dissolutions of local governments. Experience has shown that in the absence of any compelling provision to reconstitute local governments, within a reasonable period of time by democratic elections, suspended local governments will remain suspended for years and dissolved local governments will remain dissolved for decades. It should, therefore, be made mandatory for all local governments dissolved before the expiry of their term of office to be reconstituted through democratic elections, within at least six months of dissolution. To obviate the possibility of higher level governments taking over even essential functions of a local government at the slightest pretext, a broad indication of powers and functions and inter-governmental relationships needs to be made in the Constitution.

The constitutions and laws can provide only the bones of local government. Application and people's attitudes must provide the real substance. What are the conditions that society must provide to ensure effective decentralisation? Firstly, local government, as we have seen it, is essentially a power-sharing mechanism. It is not reasonable to expect a national regime, that feels its own legitimate powers to be threatened, to undertake any experiments in power-sharing. Thus the most basic need for a successful local government is public security and order, the absence of rebellion or civil war in the State.[9]

Secondly, expecting an elite ruling group, relatively unchallenged in its position, to share its power voluntarily, can be asking for the moon. How can a national government and party, faced by no overt challenger, put through a programme of political decentralisation, which seems to go against the interests of all its individual members, from the Minister down to the humblest bureaucrat? Resistance to change is built into the structure of administration itself – consciously and unconsciously, politicians and officials have a natural tendency to centralise power in their own hands and to resist measures of decentralisation.[10] They can give a thousand reasons as to why they are the most suitable persons to hold that power and how, given an opportunity, local governments would squander it away. If faced with a government strategy to decentralise, they may at best opt for a management approach, which concentrates on defining organisational linkages and structures of partnership between central and local officials. Given this resistance that has to be anticipated, a strong commitment from national leadership is the next prerequisite. They should not treat local government as one more programme for rural development,but accept it as an effective instrument in local governance. Without a strong political will, an autonomous local authority, even if there is one, will always remain the weaker party in any conflict with a nationally based department or party functionary.

The third prerequisite is strengthening the poor, so as to protect them from the exploitative behaviour of the rich. The power structure that exists today in most rural areas is likely to exploit the poor, with or without local government. If there has to be genuine participation of the poor in local government activities, then steps must be consciously initiated to strengthen the poor. These steps must include redistribution of assets through an effective implementation of land reforms (as was done in the Indian State of West Bengal), development of common property resources, efficient public distribution systems, etc.

Fourthly, it must be recognised that the powers and functions of local governments not only need guidance from above, but they also have to be defended against erosion stemming from outside.[11] The need to build up a "local government sector" within every higher level of government, which understands decentralisation, is committed to its aims and is able to defend it, requires no emphasis. An association of local governments, operated by the local authorities themselves, can also play a supplementary role in expressing the corporate interests of the entire sector.

Another key element in the success of any decentralised system is the need to reorient both the bureaucrats and the senior politicians at the central/provincial levels, from an attitude which is centralising, control-oriented and populist to one of sharing authority through regular institutions of democracy. A Minister or a Member of Parliament may gain easy popularity by saying in public that local governments need not be strict in tax collection or a by-law enforcement, but that can push the local government to near bankruptcy. Since local government functions cannot, by their very nature, be separated from their sphere of interest, local representatives of higher-level governments need to be involved in and be made more sympathetic to the needs of local governments, if necessary through a process of training and fresh institutionalisation. The retraining of officials, who have moved from the national civil service to work within a local government, comes a close second to this vital need.

Finally comes the need to train local government representatives themselves for their new role. The most interesting interface between the political leaders and the bureaucracy is always at the lowest level of government. Many Zilla Parishad members in India see the new system mainly as an exercise involving transfer of power from a reluctant bureaucracy to political leadership at the district level. Therefore, they probably consider it necessary to be somewhat assertive or even abrasive in their dealings with the bureaucracy. As a Zilla Parishad member in Maharashtra once explained, "When a man gets his chair, he has to do all such things whether he likes it or not. If I say no to anybody, then he will say, 'If you cannot do just one little thing for me, then what is the use of being in this chair'?"[12] The enthusiasm and impatience of a local politician, usually brought about by such local pressure, need not, and mostly will not, meet with a favourable response from the civil servant, in whose eyes the intention of a politician is always suspect. In the National Academy of Administration at Mussoorie, which trains young recruits to the Indian Administrative Service, the allottees to Karnataka cadre were treated with the utmost sympathy by their colleagues, as these young men and women would have to work with local politicians right from the start of their career. Contrary to these fears, there are also numerous cases of senior civil servants, who still cherish their days in a rural posting, working hand in hand with local politicians.

The politicians and bureaucrats cannot escape working with each other, especially in a democracy. It is, therefore, in their own interest to understand each other's problems and limitations, at a very early stage and in a small territory where the problems are comparatively easy and manageable. The attitudinal differences between politicians and the bureaucracy can be brought down to an acceptable level over a period of time, as both the groups gain experience in working together and managing district administration. Till then, the need to train both of them constantly, independently and also jointly, with a view not only to equipping them for their tasks but also to coexist harmoniously, will remain.

With reasonable assurance of a conducive environment for local governments, what should be an ideal structure for decentralisation? What are its functions and with what resources? These are the questions to which we addressed ourselves in the preceding three chapters. To sum up, we felt that while the exact pattern of local government below the district/county level (which in any case will be the first point of decentralisation below the State/Provincial level) should be best left to the States/Provinces concerned, the Central Governments may lay down a general criterion, which can be based on access and service, in that order. Since the essence of decentralisation is accountability of the elected representative to his electorate, the Gram Sabha or the village council should get the pride of place in any structure and should, therefore, be consciously and systematically strengthened.

A composite local government, as in Nigeria, covering both urban and rural areas, with built-in safeguards to ensure the just development of the entire area will be a more viable alternative than the Indian system of having separate urban and rural local bodies, and can also help the economic goal of decentralisation, namely, the creation of suitable growth centres. If such an experiment cannot be taken up across the board at one go, it is worth a trial at least in States such as Punjab or Kerala (in India) where the distinction between the urban and rural areas is minimal. Such a "district government" will be a political entity looking after the entire district governance, as the acknowledged third tier of the government. The elections will be held on a party basis and adequate scope for the uniform growth of administrative, local government and party structures will be provided within the democratic polity.

In allocating suitable functions to different tiers of the structure, we preferred "management by exception", implying that what the village can do for itself should not be done by the authority at a higher level, etc., even though such a principle cannot be put into strict practice in any society, for the time being. Until the local government system grows into a position of strength, the allocation of functions has to be on the basis of local conditions and mutual negotiations. While the management of resources such as land, water, forests, etc., provision of basic minimum needs such as education, primary health care, etc., village industries and anti-poverty programmes are subjects which are usually entrusted to local governments, the question of entrusting rural safety also to local governments needs favourable consideration. The key function of a local government should, however, be decentralised planning for its own development, taking into consideration every possible local aspiration. We noted that the decentralised planning model adopted by Karnataka is worthy of emulation.

In addition, the mechanics of the planning process should be so modified in developing countries as to facilitate decentralised planning and the integration of sectoral planning with spatial planning. To achieve this, national planning commissions should concentrate only on major items such as power projects, major irrigation, major transport involving several States and also major industries. The rest should be left to the States, without insisting on any sector-wise outlays.[13] The States should also avoid the habit of creating parastatals, taking away the functions and powers of local governments and entrusting even minor services to field agencies, for the simple reason that the nature of decentralisation through field agencies and parastatals in fact permits greater centralisation than if services-management had been decentralised to local governments.[14]

While discussing the financial resources of local governments, we noted how financial transfers from higher-level governments to local governments became necessary to meet their requirements to provide certain essential local public services, which had to be provided only by them to ensure efficiency in supply. We also felt that the internal generation of resources should amount to at least half of their total revenue receipts, despite all the difficulties in assessment and collection of local taxes. While the local governments in Nigeria and India depend almost entirely on grants from the Central/State Governments, China has a commendable fiscal system whose strength lies in the mode of tax-sharing. The system of local governments collecting the taxes and sharing it up with the higher levels, in addition to the flexibility enjoyed by local governments with respect to their own public enterprises, has injected financial strength to the Chinese local governments. If the political culture in other developing countries does not permit the adaptation of a similar system, then the next best option would be to assure constitutionally a percentage or quantum of internally generated revenues to be passed on as inter-governmental grants to local governments so that they can plan for its utilisation.

Turning to human resources, we noted that though the Communist regime in China cannot afford to break up its dual hierarchy of party and administration intertwined, the indications are that this would be attempted, to the extent possible, promoting younger and better educated persons than before. As for Nigeria and India, the post-independence administration in both these countries would have to change their character drastically to suit the developmental needs. Though bureaucracy cannot be the primary change agent, their role is to be suitably designed, so that they are able to respond to changing needs and demands. In respect of local government administration, we preferred the unified system, duly building into it the concept of mobility between different tiers. Replacing district officers (or District Collectors in India) by elected district governments was also suggested. Training not only administrators, but also the elected representatives, and utilising the available talent in the non-governmental sector could enhance the quality of the human resource potential of the local governments.

The Nigerian, Chinese and Indian models of local governments, as we saw, have their own strengths and weaknesses. While each system has its own peculiarities, there are also major trends and salient issues that emerge from the conception and operation of these local government institutions.

In the Nigerian system, executive power over departments is exercised not by committees of part-time councillors remunerated by allowances rather than by a salary, but by full-time supervisory councillors. The local government chairmen and the supervisory councillors are well paid and they have direct authority over local government departments, through the permanent staff of the council.[15] A second Nigerian peculiarity is the concentration on single-tier authorities in contrast to the most common two-tier British model. While the first one has worked in favour of the system and can be considered as a move in the right direction – since the earlier arrangements, though they had their virtues, confined service in local authorities to only those who could afford the time and expense – the second has evoked a mixed response. The very fact that the number of local governments went up to over 700 under civilian rule, as against 301 at the end of the military regime, indicates the inadequacy in the arrangement.

Many in Nigeria even now feel that the conflicting demands of popular democracy and development oriented local governance suggest a two-tier local government system.[16] The possibility of the incoming Third Republic, either increasing the number of the local governments (despite the lengthy constitutional procedure prescribed for the purpose) or increasing the number of the development areas within the local governments with a view to making them as deconcentrated offices of the local governments, cannot be ruled out. A third noticeable feature in the Nigerian local government system is the increasing presence of the Federal Government in the affairs of the local governments. This could possibly be a passing phase, as the States do not at present have elected governments of their own and there is very little difference between the Central and State regimes at present.

The strength of the Chinese form of decentralisation lies in the importance given to the economic management and the relative fiscal autonomy of the local governments. The only grassroot organ which is expected to promote "socialist democracy" is the Village Committee, which is just a mass organisation and not an organ of government. Even the fiscal autonomy enjoyed by local governments (which, unlike many other countries, including some in the "developed" world, do not depend on Central/Provincial Government grants for survival) is with a view to facilitating better economic management. However, there are at least four crucial elements which augur well for their limited experiment in decentralisation – strong political commitment, relative autonomy of the local administration in decision-making and implementation of local schemes, mass participation at the local level (as evidenced by the enthusiasm shown in village council meetings) and the availability of internally generated resources at the local level. The question whether the Village Committees will formally get integrated into the local government structure will still remain unanswered, at least during the foreseeable future.

The working Indian models, unlike in Nigeria and China, did not, till now, have a detailed constitutional back-up. They were the creations of the respective State Governments and, therefore, had their fluctuating fortunes. The biggest problem that faced all of them was their poor fiscal base – none of them can survive without adequate grants from the Central and/or State Governments (which also was not constitutionally assured, unlike in Nigeria). There had been no dearth of talk on the need for decentralisation in India, but very little action in most parts of the country, till now. Only very recently, attempts have been made to bring in a uniform system of rural local governments throughout the country through the Constitution (73rd Amendment) Act which has come into force on April 24, 1993 and hopefully the local governments would get established throughout India, in the year 1994.

The common trends that emerge from an analysis of the three countries indicate the operation of local governments fast becoming part of the developing political culture, either as a result of pressures from the people to have a say in policy-making or as a result of a possible incapacity of the Central Governments to cope with the needs and aspirations of the people. However, it has always been the Central Governments that call the tune. Hence, centralisation is still rampant. Local governments still function primarily as instruments for maintaining the control of the higher-level governments throughout their territory.

Even though each country favoured local governments with minimum controls from the Centre/State in theory, in actual fact they pursued a centralist development strategy. The goal is achieved either by surreptitiously subverting constitutional guarantees (as in Nigeria, during the civilian era) or by openly bypassing the local bodies through the creation of development agencies which are directly under the surveillance of the higher-level governments (as in India) or by a tight party control over the local bodies, at both horizontal and vertical levels (as in China). However, because of a growing awareness of the necessity and value of popular participation in government, most State Governments are now compelled to treat the local government as at least a rural development agent, though not as a regular district government. This is largely due to the general belief that environmental factors in most developing countries seem to favour administrative rather than political decentralisation at the local level,[17] a view held even by the World Bank not too long ago. The poor quality of political leaders, the shortage of trained and qualified bureaucracy, the generally low status accorded to local governments and the resultant corruption and poor performance have left even the local people unenthusiastic about local governments.

Despite all these ground realities, it is difficult to disagree with the view that greater decentralisation and democratisation is needed not only for development but also for fulfilling the needs and aspirations of the people. When highly centralised unitary States all over the world are now facing the grim prospect of disintegration, time has perhaps come to view decentralisation as an effective means to achieve national integration. Contrary to popular thinking, a loose federation of largely autonomous units may perhaps be in a better position to contain separatist tendencies and ethnic pluralism within the federation than a strong central authority. But care must be taken to ensure that this "functional autonomy" does not infringe free trade and industry or create artificial economic barriers, as it would otherwise result in defeating the very purpose for which decentralisation was recommended. Care must also be taken to ensure that the system does not degenerate into self-centred localism, with each locality demanding a share of each infrastructure.[18] Both these can be achieved by a careful decentralised planning in which all the tiers of government participate and have an open exchange of views, before actually finalising the national plan.

Finally, what is the route to decentralisation? Luckily in most developing countries, decentralisation has always been on the agenda. Even Nigeria, rocked for many years by civil war and applying different types of local administration in its different regions, has always kept alive the debate on local government. Transparency and accountability in public administration – especially accountability to democratic representatives – are still seen as new concepts which will take time to establish themselves before they can be practically applied[19] in many countries. A good bureaucrat is unhappy with the system of decentralisation, because it would mean more meetings, more discussions, more people to answer to and justify his actions and less time to work. A bad bureaucrat is also unhappy because the system will act as an additional (and effective) check on him, which will mean that either he has to improve and change his methods or he has to buy up the opposition, which will be costly. The resistance of the bureaucracy, though understandable, has to be gradually won over.

The centralised State will, therefore, have a difficult path to tread to reach the goal of decentralisation. May be it has first to offer a deconcentrated administration as a substitute and find it rejected by the people over a period of time. In the end, every country has to find a form of decentralisation, adapted to its own political culture and environment, as there can be no standard model to imitate. Whether the end product will be democratic, with attended party systems, etc., or whether it will be a mere decentralisation within the single-party system will again depend on the political culture of the country concerned. How long this process will take and whether the transition would be peaceful and smooth are questions we may have to leave for the historians to answer.

It looks, however, that the journey will be neither short nor easy and till the destination is reached, well-meaning politicians, bureaucrats, academics and even intelligent public have a duty to keep the flag of decentralisation flying, as decentralisation is inevitable in any human society. Decision-making over substantial public resources will have to be placed in the hands of local representatives sooner or later. The method of application of this principle can be flexible and can justifiably vary from culture to culture. Even classical models of local government may be imperfect in that they do not give adequate representation to all classes and local groups. The Central and State Governments are run by an elite and so will be the local governments. However, this will at least be a local elite, who is living with the people and who can be held responsible, if not now, at least over a period of time.

Some people believe that "excess of everything, including democracy, is injurious. Systems do collapse due to their own excesses,"[20] and, therefore, feel that centrifugal forces would somehow come into play whenever the central authority is weak. The happenings around us in the East European countries lead us to the contrary. Democracy cannot be worked by 20 men sitting at the centre. It has to be worked from below, by the people of every village.[21] It requires that everyone should realise his or her own duties and responsibilities. As Gandhiji once said, "There is no human institution but has its dangers. The greater the institution, the greater the chances of abuse. Democracy is a great institution and, therefore, it is liable to be greatly abused. The remedy, therefore, is not avoidance of democracy but reduction of possibility of abuse to a minimum."[22] This is what decentralisation must aim at and work for.

NOTES AND REFERENCES

1. Dele Olowu, *Strategies for decentralisation within developing countries*, University of Lagos Press, 1988.
2. George Mathew, *Evolution of the federal principle at the local government level*, Institute of Social Sciences, New Delhi.
3. M.J. Campbell, *Towards a comparative theory of local government*, University of Lagos Press, 1988, p. 8.
4. *Ibid.*, p. 9.
5. Frances Forx Piven, quoted by Harley Boulay, "Social control theories of urban policies", *Social Science Quarterly*, Vol. 59 (5), March, 1979.
6. U.C. Agarwal, "New awareness on Panchayati Raj", *Economic Times*, Bombay, 17-11-1988.
7. Ashok Mehta committee report, 1978.
8. L.M. Singhvi committee report, 1986.
9. Philip Mawhood, *The politics of decentralisation : Eastern Europe and Africa*, 1990
10. *Ibid.*
11. *Ibid.*
12. V.R. Gaikwad, *Panchayatiraj and bureaucracy*, NIRD, Hyderabad, 1969.
13. Dr. D.M. Nanjundappa, "Radical change in planning process necessary", *Times of India*, Bangalore, 1-10-1988.
14. Dele Olowu, *op. cit.*
15. R. Wraith and M. Dent, *The British legacy of local self-government in West Africa revisited"*, University of Lagos Press, 1988, p. 35.
16. Dele Olowu, *Developments in Anglophone West Africa*, University of Lagos Press, 1988, p. 305.
17. *Ibid.*, p. 306.
18. Biplab Dasgupta, "Panchayati Raj in West Bengal", *Kurukshetra*, February, 1989.
19. Philip Mawhood, *op. cit.*
20. U.C. Agarwal, *op. cit.*
21. Gandhiji, *Young India*, 18-1-1948.
22. Gandhiji, *Harijan*, 7-5-1931.

INDEX